EXPLORING CAREERS IN MUSIC

by

Judith Feder

The Rosen Publishing Group, Inc.

New York

To the memory of my grandmothers

Published in 1982, 1984 by the Rosen Publishing Group, Inc.
29 East 21st Street, New York, N.Y. 10010

Copyright 1982 by Judith Feder   213995

Second Printing

Library of Congress Cataloging in Publication Data

Feder, Judith.
  Exploring careers in music.

  (Careers in depth)
    1. Music—Vocational guidance.   2. Music—
Economic aspects.   I. Title.   II. Series.
ML3795.F4 1982   780'.23   82-9024
ISBN 0-8239-0557-8   AACR2

Manufactured in the United States of America

About the Author

Judith Feder was born in New York City and grew up in White Plains, New York. She received her early musical training as a pianist and played cello and percussion with school music groups. The conductor of a community chorus urged her to study singing while she was still in high school. She began her vocal training in earnest after her sophomore year of college, when she met her present teacher, Adele Addison, at the Aspen Music Festival.

Ms. Feder is a summa cum laude graduate of Princeton University. She majored in History, pursuing her other great interest, the history of architecture and design. While at Princeton, Ms. Feder was an active performer, appearing as soloist with the university's choral groups and orchestra. She performed extensively with Princeton's early music group and gave the first performances of numerous works by Princeton composers.

Since graduating from Princeton in 1978, Ms. Feder has made her home in Manhattan, where she works, studies and performs. She has appeared in opera, oratorio, recital and chamber music concerts throughout the New York metropolitan area, and has given recitals in Canada and Central America.

Contents

Chapter 1

Introduction

A career in music—what images does that phrase conjure up for you? All of us can think of a dozen or more of music's superstars, standing before the footlights acknowledging wild applause. That's one kind of career in music. But what about the people who make sure those footlights shine, or the people who make the recordings so that you can listen to your favorite star whenever you want? What about the teacher who gave Ms. Superstar her first piano lesson, or the people who write the songs she sings?

The music world is far more complex and diverse than most of us realize. Musical careers vary as much as do musical styles. Music-making takes place in classrooms, churches, and hospital wards as well as recording studios, nightclubs, and concert halls. A career in music can be part-time, full-time, or more than full-time. You can work for an organization or you can be self-employed. You may be in school for years studying music, or you may break into the music business with a minimum of formal training. The possibilities are numerous if you know what you want and you've "got what it takes" to be successful.

In writing this book, I have three major tasks to accomplish. First, I hope to give you a better idea of the many kinds of careers in music that are open to you today. Some of these fields are expanding, with new job opportunities all the time; many are extremely limited and competitive. Some may involve aspects of the music world with which you are totally unfamiliar, and some may not be relevant to your interests and aspirations. However, my goal is to show you how much choice you do have and perhaps to open your eyes to wholly new career possibilities.

Second, within the context of each career discussion, I will give you an idea of the necessary criteria for success. These include your musical talent and background, your training, your ability to establish a good reputation and to gain experience in areas that will help you to advance in your career. Fulfilling these criteria is not a guarantee of success, but you should be able to get a more realistic idea of your chances in a given career if you know what the prerequisites are.

Third, I would like to give you a sense of the life-style of young musicians and people in music-related careers today. "Life-style" includes how much you will earn, where you will live, and what you may have to do to make ends meet in a very competitive business. We will look at free-lance life-styles and life-styles that involve you in several different ways of earning money through your music simultaneously.

This book is *not* about superstars. You can read about music's stars in any magazine or newspaper, watch them in specials on television, or write to their record companies and receive a promotional packet with pictures and biographies. Superstars make the news, but they do not make all of the music. They are an infinitesmal percentage of people with careers in music.

The "stars" of this book are the people who are working—sometimes struggling—to earn a living doing the thing they love best: being involved with or making music. If you choose a career in music, you may become a superstar, but it is far more likely that you will spend your life in one of the professions described in this book, making a good living but hardly amassing fame and fortune. Even if you do become very successful, it will only be as a result of a period of hard work, stiff competition, and often only moderate financial rewards.

The music business is tough—for many reasons. In most music-related professions, there are far more qualified people than there are jobs. Much of the performing profession operates on a free-lance basis, so that in a sense most performers do not have steady jobs. There is "politics" in the music business: certain people become very popular and others fall out of favor, often with no apparent rhyme or reason. The high visibility of the superstars creates unrealistic expectations for many aspiring musicians. The fact of the matter is that for the most part music is not a high-paying profession.

At the same time, many people go overboard in their dire predictions of how impossible it is to break into music. While researching this book, I spoke on the telephone with an employee of a large record company. I explained that I was writing a career guide for high school students interested in music. "Poor misguided souls!" was her reaction. I think that was very definitely an *over*reaction. An old music teacher of mine had much better ideas on the subject. "When my students tell me they want to go into music," he said, "I do everything I can to discourage them. I tell them how tough it is, how unbelievable the competition is—everything. If they're still determined after all that—they probably have what it takes. You should go into music if there is nothing else you can or want to do with your life."

Think about that statement before you read further, because this book addresses itself to just those of you who wouldn't be dissuaded by my music teacher's arguments. I could not and would not try to persuade anyone to go into music professionally claiming that it is a wide-open field. That would be unfair and untrue. Nor could I tell you that you are likely to have a successful career in music if you are only beginning to be interested in it now. Music is not a profession for late starters. On the contrary, most people who successfully enter the professional music world have been active in music since childhood. Of course, there are exceptions. I recently attended a piano/vocal recital at which the pianist's biography proudly asserted that he had begun his musical studies at the age of nineteen. That is a highly unusual case. In many instances, young musicians are beginning to establish professional reputations by age nineteen.

Yet if my purpose is not to persuade you to go into music, neither is it to discourage you. I am a musician myself, and, while it's not an easy road, there's nothing I'd rather be doing. I want to present a realistic picture of the difficulties and complexities of the music profession while at the same time showing you how exhilarating, creative, and fulfilling a career in music can be. Further, I want to explore some avenues for working in music that offer more employment opportunities and less fierce competition than others.

We'll begin our exploration of careers in music in an area that is close to home—music education. Many of you, even those who now aspire to performing careers, will find that teaching in a public or private elementary or secondary school offers the most viable and secure way to be a professional musician. Many colleges and conservatories offer music education programs. With four years in an undergraduate school and perhaps two years of graduate school, you will be qualified to teach music. Elementary and secondary music education require competence in a broad range of musical skills. As a music educator, you will teach music of all kinds on many levels. You will have the potential to influence the artistic lives of your students in very important ways.

Some of you may want to teach music at the college level. In many cases you will need much the same skills and training as for elementary and secondary teaching. A very few of you may become professional music scholars. Musicologists, as they are called, seek doctoral degrees in the history, theory, and analysis of music. They go on to teach in their specialized fields at the top colleges and conservatories in the country.

Included in this chapter is a section on music therapy. Music therapy involves the use of music in many parts of the health-care profession, including work with the mentally retarded, the physically disabled, the aged, and those with learning disabilities. The training of a music therapist differs from that of a music educator, but music therapy shares many of the goals of music education in a specialized context.

With the exception of musicology, the music education and music therapy professions offer reasonably good opportunities for jobs and do not require long years of study for advanced degrees. Musicology is a limited and competitive field. If you are successful in this field, however, your colleagues will be some of the finest musical minds in the country. You will live and work in the stimulating environment of a college, and you may have the opportunity to travel and live in various parts of the world as you research and teach. We will explore this and the life-styles of all of the careers in music education.

The next chapter looks at careers in religious music. Religious music, too, is a fairly open field; there are part-time and full-time jobs for qualified musicians. We will look at church musicians—organists and choir directors, and synagogue musicians—cantors. Training for a career in religious music can be rigorous and lengthy, as you will see. Church and synagogue musicians are generally not highly paid because most religious institutions are not rich. Yet a career in religious music can be very satisfying. It allows you to give expression to spiritual and creative feelings and provides you with an opportunity to enrich the lives of members of your congregation through music.

The business of music is the subject of Chapter IV. Arts administration, management, publicity, promotion, and the recording industry are all part of an essential support structure, without which performances would never take place. There are jobs in nonprofit areas, such as the administration of an orchestra or opera company. There are also jobs with profit-making companies such as management and promotion firms and record companies.

The business of music takes us higher on the scale of job competition. This is a glamorous world, bringing you into contact with famous artists in brilliant settings. Many qualified candidates seek each job that opens up. A business degree is an important credential for many jobs in the business end of music. Big money goes into performances, and big money can come out of them. People in administrative and managerial positions must know how to handle that flow of funds.

In this field you will also earn more money than you would in either music education or religious music. You will earn more, that is, when you are able to work your way up from an entry-level position. In order to do this, you may have to work for a variety of organizations in various parts of the country, gaining different kinds of experience and adding professional credits to your academic credentials.

A career in administration, management, or the recording industry will be very demanding—often more than full-time. At some level, everyone in this business has the same task: to make sure a performance or a recording or a whole season of music comes off without a hitch. Your job is not finished until you've gotten all of the bugs out of the system, and you can't be sure of that until the performance is over. Deadlines, artistic temperaments, and the many and often divergent interests that help make any performance happen—these are some of the things with which you will work on a daily basis.

Chapters V and VI deal with the heart of the music business, the world of the creative and performing artist. These are by far the most competitive of all music professions, and the stakes are the highest. Composers, songwriters, conductors, and performers potentially earn far less or far more than any other music professional. I devote a good deal of discussion to these professions for several reasons. One is that composing and performing are so central to our understanding of music and the music business. All other music-related professions in some way revolve around the creation and performance of music. Another reason is that most of you who are student performers and composers will, at some point or another, consider a career in the creation or performance of music. If you love to make music, it's too tempting not to. I can say with certainty that only a small number of you will be successful composers or performers. Yet I have no way of predicting who among you will succeed. If you are serious enough about music to want to make it your career, I want to give you a full and serious exploration of the possibilities.

Commercial music is the subject of Chapter V, and Chapter VI explores classical music. Keep in mind that in both chapters I focus, not on superstars, but on young professional musicians. These are people who are working hard to establish themselves professionally and expect to earn a comfortable living. A few will become very successful; others will piece together an income from a combination of performing and writing and teaching.

There are no fixed paths to success in composition and performance. Each success story is different and, in some ways, unrepeatable. What I have tried to present in these chapters is a combination of specific examples and a body of general information culled from experiences that many composers and performers shared in common.

You will see that certain patterns begin to emerge. In most cases, composers and performers begin their musical studies at an early age and have already decided on a musical career by the time they enter college. They tend to study, live, and work in large cities, where the musical life is active and they can establish connections. Most young composers and performers enter contests and competitions or apply for grants. Not only do they have a chance to win much-needed prize money, but they receive excellent exposure as well.

Those who aspire to performing careers prepare themselves for little or no financial security in the early stages of their careers. Professional expenses are high even when professional fees are not. There are travel expenses and fees to pay to management. Publicity and promotion are expensive, as are maintenance of an instrument, proper performing attire, and, in some cases, lessons and coaching sessions.

There are certain personal qualities that may contribute to your success in these fields and, indeed, in all music-related fields. "Resourcefulness" is a word that may best sum up the qualities a young professional musician must have in order to succeed. The "resources" that are the root of the word are, of course, your own resources: your talent, discipline, commitment to and love of music; your ingenuity and perseverance in seeking out job opportunities; and your ongoing effort to improve yourself and your art. Yet there are other important resources—resources outside of you that you must discover and tap. These are the resources of teachers and training; of facilities and institutions where you can study, perform, or teach; of financial aid that can help you with a project or support when you need it. Discovering these outside resources and creating a network of connections and associations in the music world are extremely important tasks for young musicians.

Music is not an art that may be pursued in isolation. Preparation and practice may be private, even lonely, disciplines. Performance and teaching, however, are pure communication. If you don't recognize the importance of other people to your music-making, you should perhaps not consider music as a career.

The negative aspect of what I'm talking about is expressed by those who say, "The music business is nothing more than whom you know and how you exploit your connections." Yes, you do have to be savvy, personally and politically, and sometimes it may seem as if saying the right thing at the right party may be almost as important as playing like an angel. Yet the positive aspect of all of this is that the network of musical connections in this country *is* truly a network. You will see it and feel its influence wherever you go. People with whom you work will become your colleagues again in the future. A teacher in Chicago will be able to give you a helpful introduction to someone in Denver or Nashville or Portland. Your involvement in music connects you to musicians and music lovers everywhere. It is up to you to recognize those connections and make them work for you.

A very wise person once said to me, "If you have to ask someone else whether or not you'll be successful as a musician, you might as well quit right now. You'll never make it unless *you* know that you can make it." In any career in music, you must learn to be your own best critic. That is a two-step process. First, you must be able to define musical excellence for yourself. You must sharpen and refine your hearing and your thinking so as to make meaning out of the infinite variety of music you hear. It is not enough simply to know what you like. You must be able to articulate the reasons why you like certain music, why you believe it is good. Once you have arrived at a defintion of musical excellence, you must accomplish the even more difficult task of discerning when you yourself meet the standards you have set—and when you don't.

Music is a solitary discipline but a communicative art. It poses an endless series of questions and problems and provides endless joy and satisfaction. It requires technique and inspiration, study and spontaneity. The music world is not only a world of creation and performance, but of teaching, healing, worshiping, and money-making. Let's explore this multifaceted world of music and musical careers.

Chapter **II**

Careers in Music Education and Music Therapy

If you are thinking about a career in music, the people who most readily come to mind as role models are probably those who have made it to the top of the music profession—the great conductors and soloists, the principal players of the major symphony orchestras, jazz, rock, and pop stars. Yet it is more than likely that you will find *your* professional niche, not in performing, but in some aspect of music education—teaching in private or public primary and secondary schools or in a conservatory or college.

This chapter examines the field of music education: the training you will need; finding a job; what that job may entail; the advantages, disadvantages, and particular demands and rewards of teaching music. We will not, at this point, discuss teachers who work out of their own studios, teaching private students an instrument or singing. Such teachers often combine teaching with an ongoing performing career or are former performers. As such, we will discuss them in chapters dealing with performing careers. We'll discuss primary and secondary school teaching first and then look at college and conservatory teaching. In this chapter, we will also look at the field of music therapy, which is often used for very specialized educational purposes.

Certain schools require of their teachers more formal training and certification than others, and there is a broad range of salaries and benefits at various kinds of schools. You should keep these factors in mind, because the kind of job you seek will certainly influence your choice of a college or conservatory at which to train and study. Private schools, for instance, may hire music teachers who have only a bachelor's degree, but they often pay lower salaries than do public schools. Some colleges look for teachers with competency in a wide range of musical subjects, and some look for teachers whose expertise lies in a very narrow field of study. We will discuss each of these kinds of positions in the course of this chapter.

Colleges and conservatories offer many kinds of music programs. For the purposes of this discussion, however, we may think of two general courses of study: applied music (performance studies, music theory, composition) and music education. A "music ed" program will provide you with the necessary degrees and certification to teach in a public school or college. Private schools do not always require a music ed degree, and conservatories may waive formal training requirements for teachers with sufficient reputation and experience in their field.

A music ed program will give you education courses and a background in the many aspects of music you may be called on to teach —history, theory, instrumental music, choral music, conducting. Music ed majors must become familiar with all orchestra and band instruments, although they usually concentrate on one instrument or family of instruments (woodwinds, strings, brass). In fact, some students who plan a performing career elect to take a music ed program as a kind of safety net, in the event that they are not able to find performing jobs.

Of course, that safety net does not guarantee you a job in music education. A college or conservatory offering a music ed degree usually receives notice of job openings for teachers. A teacher with whom I spoke had maintained a close relationship with his high school music teachers while at college; he ended up teaching in his home town on their recommendation. Doing your own legwork— sending letters and résumés to schools and school systems—can never hurt. Private schools may be even more likely to respond to your initiative than public schools.

It is not easy to describe a music teacher's job in general terms. What and how you will teach depends on the school and community in which you find yourself. You may conduct, teach theory, music history, instrumental and choral music, even teach in a related discipline such as a humanities course. In many schools, a music teacher assumes a very public role—as leader of a marching band or conductor of school musicals. You may be asked to provide music for a community function as well. A music teacher's job certainly doesn't end with the school day. Rehearsals often take place after school hours. Some teachers conduct all-city or all-county bands, orchestras, and choruses. Some work with jazz ensembles or chamber music groups. Many teach private students, both as a supplement to their income and for the chance to work with particularly talented and interested students.

You will wear many different hats as a music teacher, but will all of them fit equally well? No one can or should expect to be equally skilled in all areas of music education. If you are a clarinet player, you won't be an expert in the violin repertoire and technique. If you love Mahler symphonies, you may be less knowledgeable about baroque music. A music ed degree offers basic training in all areas of the art and craft of music. If you, as a teacher, are lucky, a school system will be flexible enough to allow you to concentrate on a particular field of expertise. You may be able to develop a symphonic band or orchestra, a jazz ensemble or gospel chorus. Yet a teacher must also work to maintain and strengthen all of his or her musical skills.

A music teacher's self-education may be the most important aspect of his or her career, but perhaps the hardest to define. It requires of you an ongoing love for and commitment to music, something no one will ever teach you. It requires integrity, because, as a music teacher, you are *the* musical authority for most of the students attending your school. You decide the music your students will hear and play; this will very likely influence their future involvement with music. Your standards will become their standards. It may require patience and resourcefulness, especially in the present economic climate of budget cutbacks and deemphasis on school music programs. A music teacher has a musical and educational responsibility to one's students, and to oneself. Alfred Renino, music teacher at White Plains (New York) High School, puts it this way:

I never stopped going to live performances and I never will... I call it keeping my ears cleaned out . . . you've got to keep fresh. You go to the concert hall and you put yourself in perspective and say, "Am I still in tune?"—'in tune' in quotes, if you will. That is, am I still in tune with the Muse? Because I've observed so many performances, maybe I'm able to be aware of some of the subleties that go along with whatever I'm able to impart to kids. I study scores constantly. I bet I have as many scores in my house as I do printed books.

I think that Alfred Renino has a refreshing and wonderful perspective on his career. His attitude is one that may be even more important to private school teachers than to public. This is because, in many cases, private school teachers have to teach a more diverse group of students with fewer teaching aids and resources than public schools have available. Of course, many private schools are well endowed and have splendid music teaching facilities and a number of music faculty members. Yet many others are small schools, where one teacher may be responsible for students from kindergarten through high school age. Many schools are not able to provide their teachers with much more than a piano and a blackboard. If that is the case, you are really forced to be inventive about ways to teach music and musical skills.

Some teachers use their own instruments—guitars, recorders. Some invent homemade instruments out of pots and pans, bits of tubing, glass jars, scrap wood, and sandpaper, to name just a few materials. One teacher I know turned to her childhood experience with folk songs and musical games. She made arrangements of songs she had learned by ear as a child and used them successfully with a wide range of pupils.

There are also books on musical pedagogy—the study of the teaching of music. These are available in many public and college libraries and bookstores. You may need to invest some of your own time and money in such books, which are full of creative ideas for teaching music.

You may wish to explore the opportunities for teaching on the college level. There are college teachers of performance, composition, and of the history, theory, and analysis of music. We'll be looking at teacher/performers and teacher/composers in separate sections, concentrating here on music historians, theorists, and analysts. In some instances, such teachers also assume some conducting responsibilities.

"The college level" actually consists of many different levels. In this country, there are thousands of community colleges and junior colleges. There are colleges with religious orientation and, of course, the many four-year colleges and universities, public and private, with no such affiliation. There are also conservatories, where music is treated as a professional study. Each type of institution requires a particular training and imposes particular standards on its faculty.

At the top of the teaching profession is a very small number of teacher/scholars who study and then teach at the most prestigious academic institutions in this country. To reach such a position, you must not only have completed a doctorate in your field; you must be recognized as having made an original contribution to music scholarship. This may be a study of a work or a historical period that sheds new light on our understanding of music history, or it may be a theoretical or analytical study that refines our way of looking at a piece of music.

What I am describing here is a career in a rarefied atmosphere; this kind of scholarship is narrowly defined and often not accessible to the layman, or even to many professional musicians. As mentioned above, those who aspire to this level of teaching and research tend to study at the most rigorous and competitive academic institutions and then seek jobs at similar places.

The work of these musicologists (historians) and theorists may reach a more general public if their work becomes a standard text for courses in the history and theory of music. This has been the case with works such as the definitive biography of a composer, a collection of primary source readings from a certain period in music history, or a comprehensive and useful theory text. Another way you may know the work of these music scholars is through works of music they have edited. A music scholar may publish an edition of a piece of music with notes and explanations on the context of the piece and original performance-practice. This is especially helpful in editions of music composed prior to 1800. Before that time composers gave fewer specific indications of what they wanted, and publications were often inaccurate or pirated. Sometimes even a work that is now famous and often played was long forgotten, and no traditions as to how it should sound were passed down from generation to generation. A musicologist will go back to the original manuscript and early editions, as well as to things the composer and his contemporaries may have written or said about the piece. The musicologist will also consult treatises on music of the period and any other sources that may help to reconstruct the original circumstances under which the piece was performed. This is an important task today, when we value, as one music critic put it, "the loving restoration" of the original versions of great music. For performers who may not have the time or the ability to do research of their own, a fine scholarly edition of a piece of music gives them a minicourse, as it were, that can add greatly to their performance of the piece.

Some musicians seek college teaching positions while they complete their own studies or performance training. These are people at the level of writing or composing a doctoral dissertation or perhaps preparing for major competitions or auditions. The positions they find are most often in junior colleges, community colleges, and public colleges and universities. In these cases, such teaching positions are not seen as permanent. They are positions that enable these people to support themselves while they work toward another goal.

This situation does not hold true for all teachers in such colleges. For those who do seek permanent employment in such a school, however, the advanced training of a musicologist may be more of a liability than an asset. Many colleges are not seeking faculty with narrow fields of expertise, but people with competence in many fields who can teach a variety of courses and perhaps conduct a performing group as well. The training needed for this kind of position is closer to the training needed to teach music on a high school level. When I was in high school, I had a music teacher who had previously taught at a small state university in the Midwest. A few years after I left high school, he took a position at a local community college.

You can see that at this level it is possible to move between high school and college teaching positions.

A strong musical background from an early age is an advantage in a college teaching career, as it is throughout the music world. Some departments actually seek to hire scholars who are also performers and will continue to be active in local performing as they teach. Some teachers are hired in the dual role of lecturer and conductor of a choir or instrumental group.

Not only does performance provide a music scholar with a chance to put his or her research into practice, but it affords an important contrast to the solitary pursuit of academic research. To be an academic is in some ways to be a perpetual student. Furthermore, at this level you may be a student of uncharted territories, very much alone with your ideas. If you are lucky, you may have a circle of interested and sympathetic colleagues with whom to discuss your work or a performing group to balance out hours spent in libraries and archives.

A musicologist who recently received his doctorate and accepted a teaching/conducting position at a major university told me that he considers himself to be in the third generation of American musicologists. That is, musicology is a relatively recent academic discipline in the United States. Yet, while the field is developing and, as he says, becoming more refined and the scholarship more sophisticated, it is not expanding greatly in numbers. Both because of its highly specialized nature and because of the present situation of cutbacks in education, humanities programs in particular, the field remains small and competitive.

Throughout their careers, music scholars can expect to apply to foundations and endowments for grants to support their research, and to produce articles based on that research for publication in music journals. Publishing one's work is essential in every academic discipline. Not only is it necessary to establish and maintain a position in the field, but it is an important way to communicate with one's colleagues and learn about their work. Grant-supported research can be exciting and fulfilling; it may provide the opportunity to live and work in a foreign country, perhaps using old and rare books and manuscripts.

At the same time, there can be a certain lack of security about needing to publish, as well as relying on grants. Publishing is simply not a money-making proposition. The exceptions to this would be a book that has a more general public interest or an edition of music that is widely performed. Grants are wonderful when they come through, but they don't always. No one should enter the world of music scholarship thinking to make a lot of money; even the money to support essential research may be limited.

Teaching salaries do vary. Some professors are appointed to endowed positions and can earn more than $30,000 per year. Many teachers in starting positions earn less than $15,000. Often an elementary or secondary school teacher earns more than a college professor. Public school systems provide regularly scheduled pay raises, which can add up if you stay in one position long enough. A public school teacher may eventually earn $25,000 or more per year while the salary of a college professor hovers around $20,000. This is certainly less than you could earn in many other professions with a comparable amount of schooling.

You can find out about college teaching opportunities through a comprehensive list published jointly by and available to members of the College Music Society (CMS) and the American Musicological Society (AMS). This publication is called the *Music Faculty List* and includes positions of all kinds in schools of all sizes. In addition, some schools circulate their own notice of job openings, which your college may post. If you are studying music at the graduate level, you will probably belong to a society such as CMS or AMS, and you may attend their conferences. This can be a good place to find out about jobs, and even to arrange for preliminary interviews.

The interview process for college teaching jobs has several levels. You are judged, of course, on your academic credentials and performance. How you come across in the personal interview is important, and, in some cases, how you relate to other faculty members you may meet. For certain jobs, your publication credits are crucial, as well as the status of current and future research and article topics.

If you apply for a job that includes conducting or instrumental teaching, you will be given an audition. A conductor will be given from fifteen minutes to an hour to meet and prepare a group to perform a piece. The choice of music will probably be left to you, so that you will be able to choose a piece that you know well and that you feel shows you off to good advantage. A teacher will probably be observed giving a lesson.

You will be at a great advantage in applying for teaching jobs if you have some prior teaching experience. Many graduate students are able to get jobs as teaching assistants, helping a professor in a large lecture course and in some cases teaching introductory courses on their own. Not only is this an excellent way to earn money in graduate school, but it allows you to experience teaching firsthand and to work out your own style and philosophy of teaching before you take on your first full-time assignment. Although teaching while in graduate school may add a heavy burden to an already crowded schedule, it may be one of the most valuable educational experiences you will have.

If you are seeking a college teaching position as a full-time career, there can be many advantages that might not be readily apparent to you. Particularly if you teach at a school with a campus and campus life, you can become part of an interesting and supportive academic community. Many schools are able to offer subsidized housing to their faculty; excellent health and insurance plans are often available. Some schools offer free tuition to the children of faculty and staff.

If you teach full-time at the college level, your schedule will be far more flexible than in other kinds of careers. This has many advantages, particularly for two-career families. Your teaching schedule will often be concentrated into two or three days per week. The preparation required for each class varies; if the subject material is something you are currently researching and working on, you may need very little preparation time. For other classes that you have taught before, one or two hours of time before each class may suffice. A class you are teaching for the first time may require nine or ten hours of preparation for each teaching hour; however, this is a one-time commitment.

Time not spent teaching or preparing to teach will be taken up in part by administrative duties, meetings with students, grading papers and exams, and so on. This still leaves you with time to pursue your own projects and other activities. Much of that time will be devoted to research and writing, essential to your professional life. Yet you may also be able to devote time to practice and performance, to your family, or to any nonmusical interests you may have. Your life will be organized around an academic calendar, with several long vacations per year, including the big summer break.

Travel abroad will figure greatly in your life if your specialty is anything but American music. A friend of mine, himself a musicologist, spent several years in Scandinavia as a child while his musicologist father studied the life and work of a famous Danish composer. As a graduate student, my friend spent a year in Italy researching his dissertation. Another musicologist, with whom I attended school, has returned year after year to a remote corner of Russia, where he studies the music of that region. If you have a particular love for a certain part of the world, you may consider choosing a research topic that will allow you to spend time living and working there.

All of this, of course, may have to be worked out in conjunction with the needs of your spouse and family. I mentioned earlier that teaching college music can give you the flexibility to share and balance family responsibilities if both wife and husband work. Academic families do tend to be two-career families, often for the basic reason that two incomes are needed. Your husband or wife may also teach, but he or she may have a career with a less flexible schedule than yours. If you are offered a position that requires you to move, will your spouse be able to find a job in the new location? How will your children adjust to the move, or to living abroad for a year while you do research? These are questions you will undoubtedly face if you choose an academic career. It is wise to give them some thought before you are confronted with difficult decisions that must be made under time and other pressures.

Opportunities to teach college music exist at many levels. Some colleges look for teachers with overall musical competence, on much the same level as high school music teachers. Other schools look for serious music scholars who have completed years of study and a doctoral dissertation on a narrowly defined subject. At any level, there is stiff competition for jobs. You must be prepared to relocate if you get a good job offer in another part of the country. You must also realize that college teaching is not a high-paying field. A full-time college professor with a doctorate will certainly start his or her career earning less than $20,000 per year.

Despite these drawbacks, there are many advantages to an academic career. You can get involved in the many interesting aspects of college campus life. Your schedule will be flexible, with generous vacations. You will be able to pursue your own research projects and to travel and live abroad if your work calls for that. You should consider a teaching career not only if you love and want to spend your life in music, but if you have a strong desire to communicate your love of music to others. Your desire to acquire knowledge about music should be equaled by your desire to pass that knowledge along. It is great *teachers* who inspire great scholarship. That is both the challenge and the reward of teaching.

The challenges and rewards exist at the level of elementary and secondary school teaching as well. The length and type of training you seek will determine whether you teach on a precollege or a college level. Another factor must be the age of student with whom you wish to work; this in turn is related to the kind of teaching you do. On a precollege level, you may be in a position to give young people their first and only exposure to the world of music. At a college level, you will probably work with students who have already demonstrated a strong interest in music and wish to pursue their studies more seriously and deeply. In both cases the role of the teacher is crucial. Teaching and learning are only in part about the transmission of ideas. More importantly they represent some of the most creative and constructive ways people have to interrelate. The teaching profession is one that affirms its faith in the past, present, and future of our world. If you as a teacher can pass that faith along to your students, you will have accepted the challenge of education, and you will have reaped its rewards.

☆　☆　☆

The healing powers of music have been extolled in word and picture throughout history. The Bible, classical drama, Shakespeare all tell of music's power to beguile the troubled monarch, the forlorn lover; to alter an evil "humour" and cull harmony from discord.

We have observed and explored the relationship between music and health since ancient times. Yet only in the past four decades has music therapy developed as a formal academic and scientific discipline. Today it is possible to study music therapy in undergraduate and graduate programs at fifty colleges and universities in twenty-three states, from New York to New Mexico. A registered music therapist can then practice in a growing number of public and private institutions—hospitals, clinics, nursing homes, schools, day-care centers, and private studios.

The National Association for Music Therapy (NAMT) states that a Bachelor of Music Therapy degree is the standard preparation required to practice as a music therapist. Graduate study is available both for people who did not concentrate in music therapy at the bachelor's level but who wish to be certified as Registered Music Therapists, and for those who are pursuing supervisory jobs in the field or who wish to teach at the college level.

A bachelor's degree in music therapy places a strong emphasis on musical training—history, theory, performance, arranging, and music leadership skills. The latest guidelines of the NAMT suggest that 34 percent of the total degree program be directed toward acquiring those skills. Courses focusing on music therapy principles and the psychology of music make up about 15 percent of the degree. These courses deal with theoretical and practical aspects of music therapy; surveys of available literature, methods, and materials; and the ethics of the application of music therapy to major areas of human health and welfare.

Those major areas of concentration are: (1) development disabilities; (2) mental health and illness; (3) physical disabilities including neurological impairments, orthopedic handicaps, and sensory impairments; (4) geriatrics; (5) behavior disorders; (6) learning disabilities; (7) disadvantaged conditions; (8) delinquency and corrections; and (9) substance abuse. The list indicates the wide range of health concerns that music therapy encompasses. Music therapists address these concerns in their work in psychiatric hospitals, mental retardation centers, physical disability hospitals, schools for the blind and deaf, community mental health centers, day-care centers, special education schools, geriatric centers, special services agencies, and substance abuse centers. Therapists who are also music educators may work in school systems, a field with increasing opportunities. In addition, some music therapists work with clients in their own studios, often on the recommendation of a psychiatrist or other doctor.

There are two other important parts of the Bachelor of Music Therapy degree. Fifteen percent of your course work must be done in behavioral, health, and natural sciences courses. A course in abnormal psychology is required, as are courses in human anatomy and the exceptional child. For the rest, it is often suggested that the music therapy student concentrate on a limited number of areas, such as special education, family therapy, aging, behavior modification, and drug abuse. Study of scientific research methods is required, and courses in computer science are recommended.

The second part consists of a practicum and internship, in which a student observes and has the chance to practice music therapy in context. The practicum, which comes before an internship, must cover three disability areas (such as mental illness, neurological disorders, drug abuse) and should parallel course work. The internship is a six-month clinical experience in an institution approved by the NAMT and follows the completion of all other course work.

The Bachelor of Music Therapy is an intensive and directed program of study, combining theoretical and practical skill-building that will prepare you to practice music therapy immediately on graduation. It is a full program; there is some room for electives, but the NAMT suggests that students take courses in allied fields, such as dance, art, and drama. The bachelor's program takes a full four years to complete. For this reason, it would be to your advantage to know that you want to pursue a music therapy program before you enter school. That way you will be able to start on your course work in the first semester. Your choice of college will be affected as well, since only a limited number of schools offer the program.

If you don't get a Bachelor of Music Therapy degree, some graduate schools offer certification programs to qualified students. In order to enter that program at Teacher's College at Columbia University in New York, you must have fulfilled all of the music requirements prior to admission. That means you probably would have to have obtained a music degree of some kind, whether in performance or education. In addition, the college recommends that you have completed the required courses in the behavioral and natural science areas.

The certification program, then, covers only the music therapy and psychology of music courses, and the internship. Teacher's College outlines a sample full-time schedule that allows for certification in three semesters (including a summer semester) plus the six-month internship.

Once you have been certified, you can look for a job in any of the institutions mentioned earlier. There are also organizations other than the NAMT that you can contact (see Appendix A). Many job openings will be with state and Federal institutions. This means that you would become a civil servant and be able to take advantage of the salary and fringe benefits offered by the government. Salaries vary according to location and the extent of your training and experience. As the field develops, there are a growing number of higher-paying executive and administrative jobs. In a first job, a music therapist might expect to earn $15,000 or more per year.

The NAMT says that it is not possible to predict employment trends but that music therapy is definitely an expanding field. There are several reasons for this. As America continues to consider health care on a national level, alternative methods of treating illness and disability are given greater attention. In the Education for All Handicapped Children Act, Congress stated that "the use of the arts as a teaching tool for the handicapped has long been recognized as a viable, effective way . . . of reaching youngsters who had otherwise been unteachable." Music, of all the arts, has the strongest base of documented evidence to prove its effectiveness as a means of therapy.

How is music used as therapy, and why is it so effective? One reason is that it is so widely applicable; it can be used in so many situations, not only to teach music skills, but to achieve nonmusical ends. It is particularly effective in the kind of therapy known as behavior modification.

Behavior modification is a therapeutic method widely used in all areas of health care today. The theory behind behavior modification is that if you can bring about desirable changes in the way a person behaves, this will cause an actual improvement in the person's well-being as a whole. The changing of external actions is seen as a means of bringing about overall positive change.

Music is used to modify behavior in a number of ways. It can be a reinforcer. This means that a patient's good behavior is reinforced or rewarded with music. The reward may be the opportunity to listen to music or to play an instrument. Involving patients in group musical activities can help them to relate in a more positive way to other people and perhaps to break self-destructive behavior patterns.

Music can help to get a point across. Think of songs you may have learned as a child about arithmetic, telling time, the alphabet. A song is a fun and effective way of teaching a lesson. Melody and rhythm make the words and their meaning more memorable. In this way, students or patients learn academic skills and musical skills at the same time. Music can also help to develop coordination and motor skills (learning to clap in time, to play a simple instrument). Related to this, music is often used as an accompaniment for teaching job skills, particularly the assembly-line type of skill, in which the rhythm of music helps to establish the rhythm of work. Music also provides a more interesting and enjoyable background for a working environment.

If you think about it, just these few examples give you a good idea of the wide relevance of music therapy to the health-care profession. A music therapist's skills can be well employed with mentally or physically disabled people, people needing occupational therapy, stroke victims, people suffering from senility, and many others. A music therapist can make a profound impact on a patient's life at a point when doctors may be of no more help.

In fact, if you've ever thought that you'd like to make music an important part of your professional life, but that you're also very much interested in nursing or medicine, music therapy may be an ideal way to combine the two interests. As we have seen, the music therapy curriculum includes a great deal of work in the natural sciences. Although it does not prepare you to be a physician, it does provide you with an understanding of how the body works. In addition, the psychology portion of the curriculum can give you insight into a whole other level of human action and interaction.

Music therapy can give you the tools to serve people in many of the same ways a doctor or nurse does, without a lot of the drawbacks of a medical career. Although a music therapist earns less than a doctor, he or she is not subject to the long hours or emergency situations a doctor or nurse faces all the time. Doctors and nurses must often work long shifts, or at night, on weekends or holidays. Music therapists do not work in a crisis atmosphere. Rather, their task is to establish a therapeutic relationship with their patients and to work steadily and carefully to effect positive change in the long run.

The National Association for Music Therapy, Inc. was founded in 1950 and is the primary organization for the promotion of music therapy and the advancement of the profession in this country. The Association sponsors annual conferences and workshops and publishes a magazine, the *Journal of Music Therapy*. It also establishes criteria for the training and certification of music therapists and encourages research to increase the scientific basis for music therapy practice while contributing to the body of knowledge of the field as a whole.

If you are interested in a career in music therapy, you can write to the NAMT for a list of schools offering music therapy degrees (see Appendix B). Your guidance counselor can arrange, also through the NAMT, for films, field trips, or guest lecturers to help you find out more about the field.

Music therapy is a field that is growing in many ways. The scientific basis for the effectiveness of music therapy is expanding, increasing its credibility as a therapeutic method. Music and other arts are being given more and more recognition as educational and therapeutic aids, and music therapists are developing new methods all the time for the application of music to the therapeutic process. The only factor that could tend to curtail the expansion of this field would seem to be an economic one. Because many music therapists are public employees or work for institutions supported by public funds, cutbacks in government money for health care affect music therapy as well as the other health-care professions.

Music therapy is an extremely creative field. As a musician, you will probably wear many hats—performer, conductor, composer, teacher; you may even invent original instruments! You will use music and musical knowledge creatively to achieve specific therapeutic ends. You may be involved in research projects that will establish new applications for music therapy. In addition to this, you will have the challenge and satisfaction of working in a health-care field and having a direct and significant impact on the health and well-being of others.

Chapter III

Careers in Religious Music

The musical life of many Americans is shaped in great part by their religious life. For them, "music" is the music of prayer. It is music they may sing or hear during worship services, or music presented by their church or synagogue at special concerts and other events.

Think for a moment about religious services you have attended and about the range of music that you have heard. Music often begins and ends a service. The congregation sings along at certain points, listens at others. Music accompanies silent prayer and meditation and may provide a bridge from one part of a service to another. Entire portions of the Christian liturgy have been set to music by some of the greatest composers. Even if we now hear much of this music in the concert hall rather than the cathedral, remember that Bach's B Minor Mass and Mozart's *Requiem* were written for church services.

Religious music today runs the gamut: traditional folk tunes, pop tunes, Gregorian chant and trope, familiar hymns, contemporary works, and the monumental compositions of Bach and his forebears and descendants can all be heard in houses of worship. A church or synagogue musician today probably has more musical leeway than ever before. At the same time, he or she has more responsibility, by virtue of the wealth of music there exists to choose from. If you choose a career in religious music, you will shape the musical life of many of your congregants, particularly if you work in an area not close to any cultural center. It is a challenging career and one with great possibilities for creativity.

Part-time and full-time positions are available in the field of religious music. The size of your church or synagogue, the extent of its music program and budget, the range of duties required of you, and your own needs and interests will determine the nature of your employment. Some churches have four or five choirs, radio broadcasts of their Sunday services, an extensive music education program, and a concert series including recitals by the church organist. In such cases, the church requires more than one full-time musician. On the other hand, I know a cantor of a small synagogue that uses no choir or organ. He is able to fulfill all of his duties and keep up his studies and performance of opera, which he hopes eventually to pursue full-time.

Part-time or full-time, the education and expertise you will need for a career in religious music are quite extensive. Let's look at church music first. At the very minimum, you must hold a bachelor's degree in sacred music or its equivalent. According to the American Guild of Organists (AGO), a 16,000-member organization that tests and certifies church musicians, a bachelor's degree or the AGO exam at that level qualifies you to be a choir master. You must be able to rehearse and direct a choir, demonstrate competence in music history and theory, and pass dictation and harmonization tests.

You can see that a bachelor's degree—four years of study of sacred music—would prepare you for certain tasks but would not qualify you to head a full and wide-ranging church music program. There is no organ-playing requirement at this level, although it would seem wise to have at least a basic familiarity with the instrument. A description of the next level of training will give you an indication of what you can and may be expected to accomplish as a church musician.

A master's degree in sacred music corresponds to the Associateship certificate awarded by the American Guild of Organists. You must play the organ at recital level to qualify. You must be able to sight-read, to realize a figured bass at sight, to play an accompaniment from a vocal score, and to transpose at sight. You must also show proficiency in composing in sixteenth- and eighteenth-century styles. You will be tested in music history and dictation. You must know details of how an organ is constructed and must be familiar with choir training and repertoire.

From these criteria, we can surmise some of the duties of a church musician with a master's degree. You would not only rehearse and direct the choir, but also choose its repertoire from the vast resources of religious music of all periods. You might compose a work to fill some musical gap in the service. You would be responsible for the maintenance of the organ and would give solo recitals as well as perhaps playing for regular Sunday services. You might form part of an instrumental ensemble for a cantata, playing the organ, the piano, or even the harpsichord. You would probably be involved in church music education programs.

A doctorate in sacred music corresponds to the AGO's Fellowship certificate. They describe this as similar to an Associateship but at a more advanced level. This should give you an idea of the wealth of practical and theoretical musical knowledge that you will need in this field. I haven't mentioned at all studies in liturgy and theology that form part of the sacred music degree. You will also take courses in other areas to fulfill college requirements that will contribute to your general educational background.

When you have completed your degree or qualified for your certificate, the AGO's Church Musician Placement Service may assist you in finding a job. The AGO is chartered by the New York State Board of Regents, and churches apply to it for help in filling job vacancies, knowing that its candidates have gone through rigorous training and examination. You also may find job listings in religious periodicals or through the music office of a diocese. Word of mouth may lead you to job openings; the music director of your family's church or one of your teachers may know of a position.

Many churches have music committees that not only determine the scope and budget of the music program but also hire musicians. The minister and members of the congregation, some of whom will certainly be nonmusicians, make up this committee. To the committee, your musical knowledge is only one aspect of your suitability for this job.

A church music director must have a good relationship with the pastor of the congregation. The two of them are in large measure responsible for the tone and format of services, and they should have compatible ideas in this area. They work together on special events as well as routine administrative duties, which would be more difficult to accomplish in an atmosphere of lack of co-operation.

The music director must also relate well to the music committee. Indeed, he or she should be on good terms with the congregation as a whole. The music committee in particular, however, must trust the director's taste and judgment so as to be able to give him or her support and freedom in making musical decisions.

The personal religious convictions of a music director may play an important role in his or her hiring. This depends on the individual church, congregation, and musician. When you decide to pursue a career in church music, you will have made certain decisions about your religious beliefs. These decisions will almost certainly guide you in your choice of where to apply for jobs. It is up to both musician and congregation to be clear about the significance of these issues for them.

It may happen, for instance, that you apply for a job at a church or synagogue of another denomination than your own. At certain large synagogues in the New York area, which employ both a cantor and a music director, the music director may not even be of the Jewish faith. His or her musical expertise is of greater importance to the congregation than personal religious convictions.

Cantors, on the other hand, are technically members of the clergy. They can, if they choose, officiate at weddings and other occasions. Many church musicians consider themselves "ministers of music" and believe their musical and pastoral roles to be one and the same. You must decide how you wish to treat these roles and be sure you know how a prospective congregation views them.

In researching the field of religious music, I repeatedly came across a caveat directed at both congregations and musicians. Be sure to have a clear contract, in writing, between church and musician—employer and employee. The difficulty always seems to arise over recognizing that, in fact, this is an employment relationship. Churches may not view themselves as businesses, and musicians, particularly those with a religious orientation, may prefer not to come across as businessmen or women. Yet there seems to be general agreement that it is just this type of situation that makes a written contract all the more important.

For example, a church may decide to develop new programs encouraging the participation of young people in the congregation. Someone suggests that a young people's choir would be a great thing. Who will direct it? Well, the music director, of course. The music director, however, already feels overwhelmed and underpaid as his or her job stands. He or she does not see the addition of a new choir as a great thing but as an unfair burden.

Will you, as music director, be expected to provide music for every wedding and funeral at your church? How will you be compensated for this? Will you be asked to organize special concerts and activities, accompany the choir on out-of-town concerts? All of these questions are very important, for several reasons. First, you are working in a job where your personal relationship with your employers is of primary importance. There must be mutual support, respect, flexibility, and recognition that, although your job is not of the 9-to-5 variety, it does have its limits. Second, as a church musician you may be the sole employee in your capacity and one of only a very few employees of the church as a whole. You must speak loudly and clearly for yourself, because no one else will do it for you.

Once you are hired, with (we hope) a satisfactory contract in hand, how will you spend your time? Preparation for choir rehearsals may be your single greatest responsibility. It may take up to one-third of your working hours. Before you face your choir for weekly rehearsals, you must have accomplished many tasks. Selecting music is the first step. You must develop a coherent program of music for each week, working with the liturgical calendar, the hymns appropriate to the time of year, and perhaps the minister's sermon or Bible lesson of the week. You must take into account the style and texts of the music you wish to use, what extra forces you may need, how much time you have, and so on. What the congregation hears as a seamless web of music, timed just right, is the result of much time and effort on your part.

When you have chosen your music, you will need to develop an interpretation—how you want it to sound. This must be firmly fixed before your first choir rehearsal, so that you will be able to communicate your ideas to the choir with the greatest clarity and efficiency. Nothing is more frustrating or embarrassing than a poorly run rehearsal, with a director stumbling about, trying to make snap musical decisions, and the choir feeling at sea, not knowing how to respond. You develop an interpretation through study of the score and its background, comparative listening, and your own musical taste and judgment.

You may have to arrange or even compose a portion of the musical services, tasks that also fall into the category of rehearsal preparation. Maybe you've heard a popular song that you would like to arrange for four-part chorus and organ. Perhaps there is a line of the liturgy that lends itself to a musical setting. You will make these decisions and then do the writing or arranging required.

There will also be a certain amount of clerical work involved with choir rehearsal preparation. Music must be maintained and filed in good order. Choir attendance records must be kept up to date. Choir robes must be clean, in good repair, and well-fitting for each member. Some church musicians suggest that these are tasks that can and should be delegated. That is probably the ideal situation, to be sure. However, I think a church musician must expect that some or all of these tasks may be his or her responsibility.

Rehearsals themselves may take up about three hours weekly. This usually includes a two-hour evening rehearsal (traditionally Thursday nights) and a one-hour rehearsal preceding the service, but it varies from congregation to congregation. After all of your prerehearsal preparation, three major tasks remain. You must set up your rehearsal space in plenty of time for the rehearsal to begin promptly. You must conduct the rehearsal; not only each work, but the rehearsal time as a whole, deciding how much time to allot to each piece of music, how much warm-up to do, when and how long a break should be. Third, you must know how and when to work with individuals or small groups that may need special attention.

Leadership may be even more important in a rehearsal than in the actual service—and it is *very* important in the service. If you can achieve just the right balance between work and fun, your choir will love what they do and respect you. They will try hard, for the sake of the music and for your sake. They will get results and, justifiably, they will be proud of themselves and eager to maintain their good reputation. A good leader will help to inspire the kind of music-making climate that leads to better quality and achievement all the time.

A music director will also spend part of his or her work week at the organ. He or she must select weekly organ music and decide on registration (the different parts of the organ that will be used to achieve the right effect for each piece). Often he or she will have to adapt piano pieces for the organ. The organ must be maintained. If repairs are required, the music director is responsible for seeing that they are made. Last but not least, he or she must practice, not only the music of the week, but also to maintain and improve overall technique and skills. Organists must often improvise, a skill that always needs to be worked at.

For the actual service, the music director must be prepared to do a number of things. There will usually be a rehearsal before the service, and, if not, at least a thorough warm-up. Warm-ups are very important. A music director must understand what the human voice needs to do to be able to sing, especially early on a Sunday morning. During the service, the music director will play and direct, and afterwards he or she will see that everything has been properly put away.

All of this may sound like more than enough to you, but a music director has many other responsibilities. He or she must maintain a library of choral and organ music by purchasing scores and parts. This is an important and involved task, because it entails making very selective decisions from a wide range of music available. Church budgets are limited, and you must know how to spend wisely. You must be familiar with what is available, be able to judge its quality, and know how it will fit in with your current library. You may also be responsible for purchasing recordings for the library. Similar decisions will be necessary for this kind of expenditure.

Arranging special programs will be another duty. These may be. separate concerts or special events within a service, such as the performance of a Bach cantata with soloists and instrumentalists. You will arrange the program, engage the musicians needed, and work with them. There will certainly be extra tasks involved with printing programs, obtaining translations, providing for ushers, setting up and clearing away, arranging for a recording and perhaps a reception after the concert. These events can be wonderful experiences, giving you a chance to perform unusual repertoire or more ambitious works than usual, but they require a great deal of preparation and organization.

You may also be called upon to coordinate activities with other groups in the church or community. This is just a part of your commitment to the church as a whole. There will also be choir social activities and the active recruitment of new members.

Keeping and improving upon your skills is an important, self-imposed discipline for every church musician. It includes your own study and practice, but also meeting with and exchanging ideas with your colleagues. Various workshops and conferences on church music are held during the year throughout the country, some of which you will attend. The church should cover your expenses as part of the terms of your employment.

The American Guild of Organists offers a range of recommended salaries for church musicians. They base their recommendations on comparable salaries of teachers in public and private schools and colleges. In other words, a church musician can expect to earn about as much as does a teacher. A full-time church musician holding a doctorate or its equivalent may make between $16,000 and $20,000 per year. This is more or less a base figure and does not take special circumstances into account; however, it gives you an idea of what you may make in this profession. Remember that you will be paid less if you do not have a doctorate, and that you may not have full-time work in a church.

One way to augment your income is to teach. Most churches are willing to give their music directors use of the church for private teaching. This is absolutely necessary if they are teaching organ. Weddings and funerals also provide extra income, and the church should provide medical insurance and a pension plan. All told, it is not a great deal of money, but one can make a comfortable living and enjoy many of the advantages of a career in religious music.

☆   ☆   ☆

Synagogue music has two clear-cut divisions. Some denominations carry on a tradition begun in the nineteenth-century reform movements and use a choir or an organ or both in services. Although Judaism does not have the great sacred choral tradition that Christianity has, many beautiful Jewish liturgical melodies have been arranged for chorus, as well as original compositions. Synagogues that use a choir and organ hire a director/organist to lead this part of the musical service. This is rarely a full-time position. As mentioned earlier, in some cases this person may not even be Jewish. Salary will be on a level with what a church musician would be paid for an equal number of hours.

In the history of Jewish liturgical music, choral music is a very recent phenomenon. Many denominations do not include it in their services. The other, more traditional part of Jewish sacred music is that provided by the cantor, joined at times by the congregation itself. The cantor is the voice of the congregation, rendering the congregation's prayers in the most eloquent way possible. For a cantor, music is most definitely an instrument serving a spiritual purpose. A cantor is a clergyman in the Jewish religion. You can see that he or she has a very different role than would a synagogue choir director or organist.

Cantorial training requires a minimum of four years of full-time study at either the undergraduate or the graduate level. The diploma of *Hazzan* (the Hebrew word for cantor) is awarded along with a bachelor's, master's, or doctoral degree of sacred music. Courses pertaining directly to cantorial studies include Jewish music, general music, and Jewish studies, including Hebrew grammar and language, laws and customs, Bible, liturgy, and Jewish thought.

Undergraduates must meet liberal arts requirements excluding music and Jewish studies. Master's degree candidates must write an essay in the history of Jewish music or ethnomusicology. They must demonstrate command of the Hebrew language as well as a reading knowledge of two European languages. They will take rigorous oral and written exams and may be required to present several recitals. At the doctoral level the completion of a dissertation is added to the requirements for the master's.

To be admitted to a cantorial training program, you must fulfill certain academic, musical, and religious requirements. Religious first: not all programs, of course, admit women. Conservative and Orthodox synagogues do not permit women to become clergymen. Men who wish to be cantors in those denominations must be observant of Jewish law and ritual. They must have an adequate knowledge of Hebrew, Jewish history, the Prayer Book, and so on. Musically, a candidate should have a "pleasing voice," as the Cantors Institute of the Jewish Theological Seminary puts it, and should know the rudiments of music, including ear training and sight-singing. An entrance examination determines whether a candidate has the necessary academic requirements. You may be admitted to a cantorial program on a conditional basis if you are deficient in any of the educational requirements. That status will be removed when you reach a satisfactory level of knowledge in that area.

As you can see, singing ability is only a small part of the requirements to be a cantor. In fact, many congregations prefer not to have a cantor with a voice equally suited to opera or recital singing. A traditional cantor's sound is closer to a chant than an aria. The kind of singing you do will help to determine where you will get a pulpit. Whatever you choose, however, you will need innate musicality and the ability to lead people in prayer through your singing, as well as all of the knowledge you will gain in your studies.

While you are still in school, you may be able to get a part-time cantorial position. If you are training as a Conservative cantor, the placement service of the Cantor's Assembly may be able to help you. The Cantor's Assembly, based in New York, works in conjunction with other branches of the Conservative movement: the Jewish Theological Seminary, the Rabbinical Assembly, and the United Synagogue of America. The placement service is provided free of charge. It is also available to cantorial graduates looking for full-time work. The Hebrew Union College, also in New York City, trains cantors of other denominations and accepts women students. Hebrew Union also helps to place students in cantorial positions.

The Cantor's Assembly publishes a pamphlet outlining the relationship between a congregation and its cantor. It stresses the cantor's status as a member of the clergy and as an authority on all areas of Jewish music. A cantor can expect to participate in religious, pastoral, cultural, and educational as well as purely musical synagogue functions. A cantor is also a scholar and should be allowed time for study and research.

Cantors are initially hired for a minimum of two years. At least four months prior to the end of this time, the congregation should decide if they wish to renew the contract, and on what basis. The cantor can be rehired on an open-ended basis or for another set period of time, often three years. The Cantor's Assembly recommends that when a cantor has served for ten years he be offered lifetime tenure with the congregation.

Many cantors are not able to support themselves solely through synagogue work. In many parts of the country, a trend toward assimilation has caused synagogues to lose members and curtail their activities. In such cases, a cantor's services may not be needed regularly. Even if a synagogue is thriving and active, it may be small and operate on a budget that does not permit the hiring of a full-time cantor. Some cantors are able to supplement their income by teaching and by other performing, not always of a religious nature. As mentioned earlier, some people in the field of religious music do intend to pursue other careers in music; for some cantors, this may mean singing opera or other kinds of music. Trying to do both is difficult, because both cantorial work and a career in performance are very demanding. Even a part-time cantor will be involved with his or her congregation and duties. I tend to think that you really must decide on one or the other career. A cantor who accepts occasional outside singing jobs to supplement income should have no problems. But an aspiring opera singer trying to juggle demanding cantorial duties will almost certainly run into problems and frustrations.

Other cantors work at jobs unrelated to music, but on a basis that does not curtail their religious activities. If you are thinking about becoming a cantor, keep in mind that you may need a second source of income. Cantors' salaries do vary depending on the location and size of the congregation and the duties and experience of the candidate. However, it is safe to say that you could expect to earn a salary not unlike that of a church musician, that is, comparable to a teaching salary. Given the training required and the hours of work, the cantorial profession is not a high-paying one.

Although assimilation is a fact of life for many Jewish people in America today, parts of the Jewish community are strongly resisting this trend. They are exploring their culture and roots in many ways. In music, strides in the field of ethnomusicology (the study of music in different cultures) have helped interested scholars and laymen to discover more and more about Jewish music. This music has a long and rich history, and a cantor is in a unique position to study and perform it.

A cantor has the challenge of perserving a very old way of expressing religious feeling while at the same time being a successful leader of the prayers of contemporary Jews. If you find you are drawn to that kind of challenge, you may want to look more closely at cantorial training programs.

Synagogue and church music work share many of the same advantages and disadvantages. Both require substantial training and offer only moderate salaries. Both afford a certain amount of flexibility and yet demand time and energy at less easy to measure levels. Both offer more job security than many other musical careers. Neither church nor synagogue work limits you to any one part of the country, and if you find a congregation in which you are happy, you may not have to move around, except by choice. Both can be extremely satisfying musically and can give you the opportunity to shape people's musical lives in a very real way.

Chapter **IV**

Careers in the "Business" of the Music Business

There are many ways to be involved in the music business without ever picking up an instrument or singing a note. Performance is wonderful and exciting, but it's not for everyone. Performance is also only the end product of a long process of organization, administration, financing, promotion, production—the list goes on—all of which involve talented and committed people who love and know music.

Music-making has become a business, for the simple reason that it has become so costly to mount performances and, in branches such as the recording industry, it can be so lucrative. Performance may be the lifeblood of the music business, but the management and promotional industries—let's call it arts administration—are the brains and skeleton of the business, the support structure. Without this support structure, even the greatest performances would collapse in a disorganized heap.

As recently as thirty or forty years ago, the music business in America more closely resembled its beginnings than the shape it has taken on today. Traditionally, musical performances were funded and organized by private benefactors. Some performing arts organizations came under the aegis of a single philanthropist. Others had boards of trustees made up of wealthy people, all of whom may have loved music, but few if any of whom had administrative experience.

This was not a problematic situation given the small, low-budget nature of these organizations. Orchestras and opera companies did not provide full-time employment to most of their personnel, nor did they mount lengthy tours or advertising and development campaigns. All of this has changed. Today complex management organizations exist to regulate all of the logistics involved with performance. These logistics include the making of program decisions, the hiring of artists, the organizing of rehearsal schedules, and the maintenance of facilities and equipment.

Let's look at the management organization of one of the major American symphony orchestras. This management has three principal branches: (1) Development; (2) Finance; and (3) Administration. The Development branch works on fund-raising activities and helps to plan the growth and shape of the orchestra over the long run. Fund-raising is an extremely important part of any management's activities, because ticket sales, even if a season is completely sold out, may account for only 65 percent of the orchestra's budget. The Development staff looks to the government and private sources for funding. They work with the many volunteers without whom performing arts organizations in America could not exist—people who run thrift shops for the benefit of the orchestra or organize fund-raising dinners. The current budget of this orchestra is $12 million annually. Raising 35 percent of that sum is no small feat for the Development staff.

The Development staff works closely with the Finance section of the organization. The people in Finance make the day-to-day decisions about how the orchestra's money will be spent. The Finance section probably requires the least musical knowledge and the most business experience of its staff. In fact, a former member of this orchestra's management told me that she would counsel almost anyone interested in a career in arts administration to get a business degree rather than studying music. This is not to say that music knowledge is not an invaluable asset for a career in arts administration. It is more an acknowledgment that the music business is increasingly a money business. If you want to be successful in it, you must know how to manage money. We'll discuss that issue in more detail later in this chapter.

The Administrative branch of management is probably the most complex and multifaceted of the three divisions. It is also the branch that gives its staff the most contact with performers, performance, and the artistic decisions that go into the making of a season of music. The Administrative branch oversees operations: rehearsal schedules, stage and equipment needs, maintenance of the hall, orchestra personnel, and library. It also handles publicity and marketing, publishing the program book, designing and producing advertisements for radio, television, and printed media. The Administrative staff forms a direct link between the musicians and music director, the rest of the management organization, and the orchestra's board of trustees. An artistic administrator hires guest artists and conductors. He or she helps the music director to make programming decisions and must achieve a balance between artistic integrity and innovation and the realities of budget and logistical considerations.

The Administrative branch of management highlights the unique nature of the music business: that is, that it *is* a business, but it is also music. Arts administration is about the flow of money, but also about the flow of sound from stage to audience. An orchestra's management must achieve a balance between what is best for business and what is best for art. Often management and the artists with and for whom they work seem to speak entirely different languages. Anyone who can bridge that communications gap will fill a crucial role in arts administration.

Arts administration can be a 24-hour job. Your work day starts at 9 A.M. or even earlier and ends when the concert is over. It is deadline-oriented work—each week brings new concerts with their own logistical complexities and peculiarities. You can't leave something until next week if it is needed before the curtain rises at 8 P.M. tomorrow. People in arts administration—from secretaries to executive directors—become accustomed to late nights, weekends, and taking work home.

Your job becomes your unquestioned top priority in this field. Any other interests, including your own practice and performance, must take second place. Arts administration is an extremely pressure-filled profession. Yet it is also a very desirable one. The competition for jobs in arts administration is intense. What motivates people to seek careers in this field?

There are many kinds of motivation for arts administrators. It is an undeniably glamorous field, providing an opportunity to work with wonderful music and talented and famous people. Artists need management, and it is very satisfying to know you are fulfilling an essential role. When a concert comes off successfully, an administrator can take great satisfaction in the concrete results of his or her efforts. Working for music and musicians is working for a good cause, and that too is a great source of satisfaction. In addition, an orchestra or other performing arts organization occupies a central role in the community. It is a source of pride and a focal point for many activities. Working for such an organization means feeling very much at the center of one's community.

Arts administration attracts dedicated, creative, intelligent people. At the top of the profession arts administrators can earn salaries commensurate with their experience and abilities. Although performing arts organizations are nonprofit institutions, their boards of trustees recognize the importance of attracting the best people to important positions in management. Administrators in directorial positions can make well over $50,000 per year. This represents a rapid rise in top salaries over recent years, and it is a trend that cannot continue indefinitely. However, you can see that, in combination with all of the other pluses, the salary level makes a top arts administrative job a very attractive post.

Unfortunately, the salaries for entry-level positions in management do not approach the top figures. Entry-level positions pay not much more than secretarial positions, that is, around $15,000 per year. The work is very demanding, and chances for advancement within the organization are quite limited. This is because your job is usually so specialized that you are not able to gain the overall managerial expertise that would make you a candidate for promotion. To qualify for directorial positions, you need to have had broad experience, especially in financial matters. Particularly if you work in the administrative end of management, you may have very little exposure to the financial end, even though you may be closer to the artistic side of the business. The positions that involve you most with music itself may be the least advantageous from the standpoint of advancement.

How do you get the kinds of experience you need to reach the top of the arts administration profession? As we discussed earlier, a business degree (the Master of Business Administration) is a very important credential. Today it is possible to earn this degree with a focus on arts administration. Graduate programs in arts management are excellent additions to the academic scene, because they recognize that, while the study of business is important to arts administrators, different rules apply to the management of a nonprofit cultural institution than to a profit-making company. You can study arts management at a growing number of schools throughout the country, including the University of California at Los Angeles, the University of Wisconsin, Columbia University, and New York University.

Another way to gain expertise is to work for a small performing arts organization in which you might be required to wear a number of different hats, from accountant to artistic adviser. If you can rise to the top of such an organization, you'll gain exposure you would never get lower down in a larger, more glamorous management organization. Start right away: look into managing the band at the college you will attend. Find out about local groups in your community. You may do a lot of drudge work, but you will learn the business inside and out. More important, you will establish your credentials in leadership positions.

You may also have to move around a lot. People who are looking to advance in arts administration do not stay indefinitely with an organization in which they began at an entry-level position. They look for better positions with other organizations, perhaps at the other end of the country. Another factor that tends to cause a lot of moving around is the network of connections that operates throughout the music world. The manager of a major West Coast symphony orchestra moved there from a similar position with a much smaller orchestra on the East Coast. When another high-level position opened up, the manager offered it to a woman who had managed a chamber music group in a city near his old home base. A manager in a new position may also recruit people from within his or her former organization, knowing that they will be able to work well together. The point to remember is that you may have to move all over the country, especially while you are establishing yourself in this profession. That can be difficult, particularly because arts administration tends to involve you so fully in the community in which you live and work.

In the next few years you may want to look into various summer and year-round programs that can give you some initial experience in arts administration. Many organizations offer unpaid internships and volunteer positions for college students. The American Symphony Orchestra League offers a one-year, paid internship for people who have completed their undergraduate degrees. A college career placement office will have full details about that program, or you can contact the league directly (see address in the Appendix).

Up to this point, our discussion has focused far more on business than on music. In fact, if your love for and desire to be active in the world of music is your motivation for going into arts administration, you may find yourself frustrated at certain points along the way. One woman in orchestra management said to me, "You can't imagine how far away from music you can get in this business."

What she meant, I think, is that, because an arts administrator has the job of solving all of the problems and smoothing out the rough edges that might detract from a great performance, he or she may get caught up in the process of problem solving and never have a chance simply to sit back and enjoy the music. A performer must work and struggle in his or her own right, but when the time comes to step onto the stage, he or she has only one job to do. If something is wrong with the lighting or the temperature in the hall or the way the program is printed, the performer can turn to the manager and say, "That's not my problem—you take care of it." If you are in management, you can't turn to anyone else. It *is* your problem, and you must take care of it.

Stories circulate in the management profession of people who have been so turned off by the process that they turn off to the music as well. They refuse to go to concerts, perhaps as a kind of futile protest against a job that seems to run their lives. At the same time, there are people in arts administration whose interest in music is limited in the first place. As mentioned earlier, these tend to be people in the Finance departments of management organizations, people who really need no understanding or love of music to do their jobs well.

In almost any other instance, however, the more you know and care about music, the better your job will be, not only in your performance, but also in the richness of the experience for you. Of course, there will be times when the glamour and excitement of the concert hall seem infinitely distant from your desk and your constantly ringing telephone. Yet there will also be times when you will be in close enough to touch that excitement, when, in fact, you will be right in the middle of it.

If you work in Development, your musical knowledge will add immeasurably to your "sales pitch" for your performing arts organization. You will be able to speak with authority about upcoming musical plans and past achievements. In Administration, musical knowledge comes into play on many levels. In operations, you must know that different forces are needed for a Mozart symphony and a Mahler symphony. If you deal with orchestra personnel, you ought to know firsthand how it feels to perform and what the players' particular concerns may really mean. A music librarian must be extremely knowledgeable: to keep track of scores and parts, to mark parts according to the directions of the section leaders, and to be sure all of the music is in the right place at the right time. Orchestra librarians usually come from professional performing backgrounds.

In publicity, your knowledge of music will help you when you research information on a piece of music or one of your upcoming soloists. If you are in charge of scheduling rehearsals, you must understand the psychology of the performer. For instance, say you are scheduling a rehearsal for orchestra and four vocal soloists. The only time you can get everyone together is at 9 A.M. You can expect to have to smooth the ruffled feathers of singers who think their voices should still be at home in bed at that hour! What if you are assigned to greet a famous artist at the airport? What will you talk about as you drive to his or her hotel?

You will certainly need a high level of musical knowledge and experience if you become involved with actual artistic decision-making—program choices, who will conduct or play what concerto, which composer will receive the commission for a new work. Again, one of your greatest assets in such a position will be your ability to maintain a system of checks and balances, reconciling the often divergent concerns of finance and art.

☆　　☆　　☆

Working in the administration of a large performing arts organization is not the only way to be involved in arts administration and management. You may have heard of Sol Hurok, the great impresario who discovered and managed the careers of many great artists of our time. While the image of Hurok, smoking a cigar and in full evening dress, may be a bit outdated today, the field of artists' management is alive and well.

Performers need managers for several reasons. Managers are in touch with an international schedule of performances and can arrange auditions for their artists for engagements in halls around the world. Managers negotiate contracts and assist artists on other business and logistical matters. A management also provides a kind of tacit guarantee to the rest of the music world of an artist's competence. A management will not sign an artist onto its roster until he or she is ready for a full-fledged professional career. Many auditions are open only to artists represented by management; this insures that there will be a minimum standard of artistic competence among those auditioning.

Artists' management is a limited field in the sense that a single manager can manage the careers of a number of artists. Even the largest managements, such as Columbia Artists, have relatively small staffs. At the same time, there is probably more opportunity to work your way up in artists' management than in orchestral administration. You'll learn more about different parts of the business in a management office because the size of the staff means you will do many different things.

Arts administration and management are certainly not limited to classical music. There are management and promotional companies that handle pop, jazz, and rock 'n' roll artists. Producing a rock concert is an impressive feat, involving as it does such a large amount of complicated electrical equipment on top of the usual logistical details, and an overflow crowd of wildly enthusiastic fans. The financial end of nonclassical music management is different from that of classical music, because in most cases the promotion of popular music is a money-*making* proposition, rather than a fundraising and spending proposition.

Working for a record company is another way to use your

musical knowledge and work closely with performing artists. Record companies today have many branches, some dealing with financial matters and others with the actual production and promotion of recorded music.

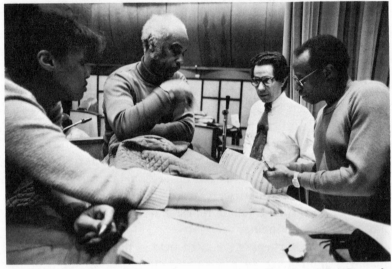

Courtesy RCA Records
A producer discusses a recording with cast members of Sophisticated Ladies, *a Broadway hit musical.*

Producers work directly with recording artists, helping them to develop their musical ideas into coherent concepts for a successful recording. Promotional people take the finished product and make sure it is played on the radio, displayed prominently in record stores, and reviewed in newspapers and magazines. They also organize tours to publicize the new album of a band or recording star.

Sound engineering is a crucial part of the recording industry. Few if any recording artists envisage their music without the near-miracles that can be worked on it from the engineer's booth. Sound engineering has developed into a sophisticated art, requiring great technical and musical skill. It is similar to film-making in the sense that, until recently, the only way to learn the art was to do it. There were no schools in which to study; you apprenticed yourself and got hands-on experience of your craft. Today more and more people seek formal training in sound engineering; in fact, it is difficult to find a spot in which you can apprentice yourself and learn in a real-life situation.

☆   ☆   ☆

The business of managing music will continue as long as music continues to cost so much and, in some areas, to make so much. It is increasingly important to have academic credentials to get a job in arts administration, management, or the recording industry. A business degree is very useful for many jobs in these professions. It is also important to have a wide range of experience in the music world. You may have to deal with the representative of a stagehands' union, the governor of your state, or a temperamental virtuoso—all in a day's work. Your own music-making will have to take second place to your top priority: your job and the music you help to make happen. The business of music is fast-paced, pressure-filled, and peopled with bright and dedicated men and women. It has its frustrations, but also its glamour. The business may dictate where you live and how you spend virtually all of your time. Yet it offers rewards at many levels. If there were no "business" in the music business, there would also be no music.

Chapter V

Careers in Commercial Music

New York is the commercial music capital of the world. That may sound like a bold statement, but I think that most people would agree with it. Nashville may be the center of the country music scene, and Las Vegas may have cornered the market on splashy nightclub acts. Los Angeles has a bustling film, recording, and advertising business. But New York has it all—from Broadway shows to formal dinner dances, from recording studios to jingle houses. For volume, variety, and quality of music-making, New York comes out on top.

Commercial music and musicians are many different things. Dolly Parton is a commercial musician; so is the guy playing bass for the background music to that funny cat-food commercial you see all the time on TV. A player in the pit orchestra of a Broadway musical or in a classy dance band are both commercial musicians. Club dates, parties, recordings, commercials, shows all provide jobs for commercial musicians. And there are plenty of job opportunities for people with top talent and versatility.

For people on the outside, commercial music is also a field where myths abound. There is the superstar myth: that "the biz" is one long string of parties, glamorous appearances, and big, big bucks for all involved. Then there is the down-and-out myth: that the commercial musician sees life (through a haze of drugs and alcohol) as an endless series of one-night stands, neither willing nor able to settle down, never quite making it.

The truth is, there *are* different levels of making it in commercial music. You see and hear the superstars all the time. The marginally successful types exist, too—people for whom gigs are few and far between and who probably need to work at other jobs to make ends meet. The majority of commercial musicians, however, who have achieved a certain level of *professional competence* make comfortable and often lucrative salaries, work steadily, and go on the road only by choice. You may not know their names or read about them in *People* magazine, but they are professional, working musicians.

Professional competence is the key to achieving success in the commercial music business at a level between stardom and struggle. A term introduced to me by a successful New York commercial musician and teacher, professional competence means living up to New York standards, which get higher all the time. It means being at home in a variety of musical styles and working situations. It means being able to perform at full capacity in pressure situations such as a recording session. Above all, it means never having to say "no" when a phone call comes offering you a job.

It's a peculiar aspect of the music business that, no matter how successful you are, you *are* dependent for jobs on those phone calls from agents, contractors, producers. If you are good, those phone calls will come, but you are, basically, a free-lancer. You must constantly prove yourself to those who hire you—by being willing and able to work jobs into your schedule, by being able to sight-read and improvise if necessary, by being competent and knowledgeable about many styles of playing or singing. Among the few exceptions to this would be the musician in a successful Broadway show or in a band that appears regularly at a nightclub. These can be steady long-term jobs—as long as the musical fills the house or the nightclub act remains popular.

You struggle, audition, introduce yourself to people who can hire you, do your share of less-than-great jobs. You build a reputation and work hard to keep it a good one. If you stick with it, you'll establish yourself in the business, developing a network of friends, colleagues, and contacts. Yet while you're getting there, the process is a solitary pursuit. You're very much on your own.

Unlike many other professions, and even other parts of the music world, the commercial music profession has no strong overarching professional organization. Of course, there is the musicians' union. All of the work we've been discussing here is union work, and you must be a member of the musicians' union to get this work. The union protects working musicians, guaranteeing that certain salary and working conditions are met. These are vital functions and not to be underestimated. However, the union does not provide a forum in which music professionals can meet, exchange ideas and information, find jobs, improve their skills, and so on. There is no specific place, for instance, for a commercial musician to learn about all the ins and outs of residual payments that you may be owed for a recording in which you appeared. You may be successful enough or foresighted enough to hire a good lawyer to help you in such matters, or you may be lucky enough to have a clear and fair contract offered to you at the start of a job. Many musicians have told me that you learn about such things only through experience. Yet the experience may include several instances of your being "burned" before you learn how to "play the game."

There are many aspects to "playing the game." First, you have to have that professional competence I was talking about before. You have to be very, very good at what you do. What's more, in a place like New York, where so many people aspire to careers in commercial music, you have to have something special. What that something is, I can't pin down exactly—call it charisma, a distinctive style, fabulous fingers, a particular way of shaping a phrase. The important thing is that *you* have to know you have it, and you must let other people know as well. As the song in a hit Broadway musical says, you have to have "just a little touch of star quality."

You also have to try to shape your career in a specific way. Find contractors and agents who like you. Make sure they know what you are doing, what you *can* do. Let them see your versatility and any special talents you may have—in sight-reading, improvising, arranging. Go out on the road, but remember that your connections at home will be less secure when you return. Each job is a building block for your career, so keep in mind what you want the building to look like.

You can help to keep your connections viable by putting together a first-class publicity package and keeping it up to date. Singers especially need excellent photos and demo-tapes as well as a polished résumé. These are all expensive items, but consider them wise investments. There is a lot of self-promotion involved in the music business. This may be a part of the profession you like less than other parts, but it's a necessary step to get you where you want to go.

The cast of Merrily We Roll Along *records the original cast album.*

Be open and aboveboard in all your professional dealings, and quietly but firmly assert this attitude with colleagues and employers. That is advice that would be well taken in any field. However, I stress it for the commercial music world because you will find yourself in so many different kinds of employment circumstances. For instance, if you are offered a job, accept it, and then receive a better offer that conflicts with the first, be honest with both sides. Find out if you can be replaced in the first job. If not, don't walk out at the last minute—honor your commitment. The old cliché is true, you are only as good as your last performance, and that includes how you perform as a business person.

On the other side of the coin, make sure that you are aware of and agree to all terms of employment for jobs you accept. Get things in writing—it's the best way to avoid misunderstandings. How many rehearsals will you attend, and for how long? What are your performance obligations? What credit will you get for your performance or material? These are just some of the common-sense questions that should be answered about any job you accept, but young, starting-out musicians may easily pass over such things in their eagerness to get work.

Certain areas of commercial music offer more employment opportunities than others, and you may be able to break in through these more easily. Big cities mean big hotels, and big hotels mean big parties. Big parties mean dancing, with music provided by live bands. In New York a successful commercial musician can play in a dance band almost any night of the year. Some bands may use musicians more or less regularly, and, of course, there are some band leaders who are very popular and appear on a steady basis. In many cases, however, these are pick-up groups, coming together for a specific gig. To be successful at this, you must be able to fit in without a hitch. You've got to know all of the music, all of the styles you may be asked to play—and know them cold. What happens if the leader gets a request and says, "OK, let's do it in B flat?" You do it in B flat, and you do it right.

Shows also offer a fair amount of steady employment to commercial musicians. You may be lucky enough to be in the pit of a hit Broadway musical and have several years' work at $500 to $600 per week. There are other types of shows as well. There are smaller musicals, straight plays that use music, cabarets, and revues. There are Las Vegas–type theater shows, not only in Las Vegas itself, but in other resorts and hotels.

Many studio players begin by playing shows. If they work hard, cultivate connections, and establish good reputations, they may work their way up to the more lucrative world of the recording industry. Whereas a band or pit musician may make between $20,000 and $30,000 per year, a studio musician may make $50,000 and more. Remember that we are not talking about stars, but about *successful* working musicians.

Jingle production is another lucrative area of the commercial music business. Jingles are the music you hear on radio and TV

A commercial recording session.   *Courtesy RCA Records*

advertisements. We'll discuss the writing end of jingle production in the section that follows, on commercial songwriting. From the performers' point of view, there is a very wide range of "making it" in jingle production. The American Federation of Musicians, the musicians' union of the United States and Canada, estimates that "in this industry... there are some 15 or 20 musicians who earn well in excess of $100,000 a year." That's 15 or 20 people nationwide. Further, "there are approximately 5,000 musicians who earn $1,000 or more in a year in connection with the production of jingles." Now, that "$1,000 or more" can mean many things—but it certainly means that fewer than 5,000 people make a full-time living playing jingles. On the other hand, it means that some, or even a good many, of those 5,000 musicians may earn up to $99,000 dollars per year.

In jingle production, the largest fees may be commanded by singers. The American Federation of Musicians' figure of "well in excess of $100,000 per year" jibes with an estimate of jingle singers' salaries made by a New York commercial musician. The top people, he said, may make $250,000 a year. Keep in mind, however, that we are talking about a very, very few people. The best people get the best work. The same players and singers may be heard on many commercials. The best commercials, in turn, are aired most often. Each time one appears, a residual payment is made to those musicians whose contracts stipulate such. You may receive many times your actual fee for making the commercial.

The figures above indicate that relatively few people make it to the top—and by top, I mean making a full-time living—of the commercial music business. The American Federation of Musicians estimates that 5,000 musicians earn "a substantial if not complete portion of their income" in the recording industry. Another 3,000 or so earn their livelihood in the film industry. These numbers may make more sense when you realize that the American Federation of Musicians estimates that only 10 to 15 percent of their 300,000 members make a full-time living at music.

These sobering figures help to explain why some commercial musicians become involved in the business end of their profession. Most contractors, the middlemen who hire musicians for jobs, are musicians themselves. They come up through the ranks, initially getting into contracting as a way to make more money. Eventually their status may change; they may give up playing altogether and contract full-time. A band musician who plays at a lot of parties may open an office that can put together a number of bands at any one time. Again, this may start in an informal way: a means of organizing the far-flung resources of free-lance commercial musicians and earning an extra fee for that organizational service.

Teaching is also a way of life for many commercial musicians. Because much of your work takes place at night, you have the flexibility to take on students during the day. There is great demand for good teachers in this field, because commercial music is not taught at colleges or music conservatories. Even jazz schools teach a brand of jazz that is often more intellectual and less marketable than what you need to make it in the commercial music business.

Commercial music demands a high degree of competence in certain practical skills. You've got to know that a *salsa* eighth note is not the same as an "r and b" eighth note, a country and western eighth note, and so on. As one musician put it, "If you're a saxophonist, you've got to know how to sit in a saxophone section and play the third harmony part without music."

A good teacher should help you to develop many of these skills. In fact, you may need more than one teacher, depending on the skills you're interested in developing. You might work with one person on your instrumental technique and someone else for theory and arranging. The reputations of good teachers spread quickly through the musical network by word of mouth. If you're looking for a good teacher, ask around. Observe your peers. If you like what one of them is doing, ask about his or her teacher. Go to clubs, listen to the bands, find out who's doing a lot of playing and if they teach as well. You have to have an idea of what you like before you can find a teacher.

In the "good old days," your education in commercial music was probably a combination of working with a teacher and picking up knowledge and experience on your own. You'd learn on the job, through both your mistakes and your successes. Professional competence was probably not something you consciously trained for; it was the natural outcome of hard work over a period of time. Today, however, things are somewhat different. There is more commercial music than ever before, but there are more talented and competitive musicians, too. There are more teachers than ever before, but that means more fakes as well as more good teachers. There is probably less opportunity to learn by doing, because so many musicians are already at a level where they can take on any kind of assignment they are given. Producers can't afford to have people learning on the job; you've got to go in knowing exactly what you're doing.

For these and other reasons, musicians and educators have begun to realize that there should be institutions that can offer music students an all-around practical training in commercial music. In New York, for example, the recently founded New York School for Commercial Music offers "a unified curriculum designed to provide singers and instrumentalists with the skills necessary" to be successful commercial musicians.

The founders and faculty of this school are themselves successful commercial musicians. They have been observers of and active in the scene for a number of years, and they know how many different elements go into a successful career in commercial music. They offer courses in theory, sight-singing and musicianship, improvisation, arranging, composition, and vocal and instrumental ensemble, among others. These courses are all taught "within the context of commercial suitability." Future plans for the school include offering courses in the business end of commercial music to help musicians with the practical aspects of managing their careers.

I don't mean to imply, nor does any school claim, that their curriculum is a guarantee of instant success in the commercial music world. Few if any musicians can bypass the stage of knocking on doors, going to auditions, building a reputation, and working and struggling to make it. Yet I do think that there is much to be said for a school founded *by* commercial musicians *for* commercial musicians, a school devoted to the fundamental and practical aspects of the workings of the commercial music business.

Singers and instrumentalists can have successful careers in commercial music. Although this career cannot offer conventional job security, a successful commercial musician will not lack work. The chances are against your becoming the next Bruce Springsteen, but you won't necessarily become the itinerant backup guitarist for a second-rate rock band, either. You will most likely make your home in New York or Los Angeles, combining work in recordings, clubs, parties, and shows with teaching. The few at the very top, especially the best singers, will make far more money than the rest. Yet, while the range of salaries is very wide, it is possible, at many different levels, to make commercial music a full-time career.

☆   ☆   ☆

In the first part of this chapter, we looked at the careers of *performing* commercial musicians. Some of these musicians compose their own music, but many perform music written by others. Some popular music composers started out as performers, although they now compose full-time. Others continue to combine composing and performing careers. I'd like to explore the songwriting profession by looking at the careers of one New York–based songwriting team: Abbott and Weeks.

Sarah Weeks and Michael Abbott are a team: wife and husband, lyricist and composer, singer and pianist, they work and live in a large apartment on Manhattan's Upper West Side. They have performed in jazz clubs and piano bars throughout the city and know the ins and outs of that world. Recently, however, they have concentrated their efforts on the very challenging field of songwriting. Their long-range goals are clear, and they are working hard to get where they want to go. The route they are taking points up their own talents and resourcefulness, but also the broad range of the songwriting field, with its pitfalls and rewards, as well as certain avenues that may make an extremely competitive field a little easier to break into.

I asked Michael what type of music he wrote. He found it difficult to say—almost any answer he gave would be inaccurate or too narrow. He felt comfortable, he said, writing in a variety of styles. I then asked a question he found far easier. "When you write a song you think is really good, whom do you want to perform it?" "Everyone," he answered immediately. I think I understand what he was getting at. Sarah and Michael want to write music that is "popular" in the sense that many people will know, enjoy, and sing their music.

Michael's answer made me think that there have been all kinds of "hit tunes." In the 1780's everyone in Vienna and Prague whistled tunes from Mozart's *The Marriage of Figaro*. When Verdi was rehearsing a cast for the premiere of *Rigoletto*, he made the tenor swear not to breathe a note of his third-act aria outside the hall. Verdi knew that if the gondoliers of Venice got wind of it, they would have made "La donna é mobile" famous before the opera ever opened. In this country, throughout the heyday of musical theater, Americans hummed, whistled, and harmonized the tunes of Gershwin, Cole Porter, Rodgers and Hammerstein, Lerner and Loewe, and others.

Today, however, "popular" music often connotes "pop" music, and "pop," in turn, connotes "commercial" music. Weeks and Abbott have had to make these distinctions for themselves as they look for and get different kinds of songwriting work and as they think about the ideal creative situation they hope to achieve. They hope their work is "commercial"—that is, that it sells and brings them financial success. At the same time, they have disregarded the advice of people "in the business" who have told them to "write dumb"—that is, to write simpler lyrics and melodies, like any of a thousand disco tunes you can hear on the radio.

To escape churning out music that might have been successful but unsatisfying to them, Sarah and Michael have turned to musical theater. They believe that writing music and lyrics in a dramatic context will allow them the freedom they want and need without passing out of the realm of what is commercially viable.

They have one musical theater project in the works (which will be produced at a major Off-Off Broadway theater) and one project "on the shelf." At the same time, they have a free-lance contract to write songs for the TV program "Sesame Street" and are finishing up a song for Woody Allen's upcoming movie.

Sarah and Michael have written jingles "on spec." That is, they have written and taped music for commercials and have submitted the tape to "jingle houses." Jingle houses are where advertising agencies turn for the music for their advertisements. A jingle house typically employs only a handful of writers who can write this kind of music with great facility. It's extremely lucrative and just about impossible to get into. Sarah and Michael were able to submit their tape only because of a connection they had. When they called several weeks later to find out if their tape had been listened to, they were told that no one got a response of any kind until at least two years had passed.

While they were disappointed, they were also somewhat relieved. Both explained that it is easy to fall into a pattern of churning out words and notes—quantity without necessarily a great deal of quality. Even if you feel it's not your life's work, if you can get a lot of money for writing jingles, or even songs for "Sesame Street," you may begin to do that kind of writing to the exclusion of other things almost without realizing it. Trying to get back to more substantial work after a stint of "hacking" can be extremely painful, Sarah and Michael agreed. The discipline required is far greater, and the financial rewards may be far less, at least in the short run.

Sarah and Michael each studied piano as kids, getting a typical grounding in the classical literature. Michael had more formal studies in theory and ear-training in the Preparatory Division of the Manhattan School of Music. Both attended "experimental colleges." Sarah went to Hampshire College in Amherst, Massachusetts, after attending high school in the Midwest. Michael went to the California School of the Arts and then Hampshire. They each majored in music, describing their training as more creative than formal. Sarah wrote a lot of poetry without making a formal study of it. Michael studied jazz piano for three years with a teacher in Boston, who he says taught him most of what he knows about music.

They made their separate ways to New York, each intent on a performing career. Pounding the pavement and accepting engagements in small clubs for little money, they were each able to get performing experience. Looking back on that time, Michael says that he found the jazz scene, at the level in which he was involved, economically depressed, a fact that he feels adversely affected his fellow musicians in many aspects of their lives.

Sarah worked as a secretary to support herself. Michael waited on tables and was eventually able to teach jazz piano. However, each began to feel dissatisfied, not only with their life-style, but also with the music they were writing. Michael wanted to work with words, even though he enjoyed the improvisational aspect of jazz piano. Sarah felt she was not progressing musically and was frustrated by that.

They began collaborating before they became close personally. Sarah gives Michael musical input, but she alone deals with the lyrics of their songs. Not only do they work in close physical proximity, but they consult frequently. Sarah will give Michael a fragment of a lyric so that he gets a sense of what she's thinking about a song; Michael will play for her a bit of melody or a chord progression with which he's working.

Sometimes, they say, they may consult each other too frequently. "We like each other," Sarah says, and the natural impulse is to share—the good and the bad. That can occasionally be bad for concentration and discipline. When they begin to make more money, they say, they'll get separate studio space.

Establishing work space may also make them more formal about their work time. Self-employed people place a great scheduling burden on themselves; no one expects them in an office or a factory, or requires a certain daily output. If you get bored or frustrated, you *can* simply put your work away and tell yourself you'll come back to it later. Sarah and Michael say they have succumbed to what I call the "going-to-the-movies syndrome"—giving up on your work at a frustrating point and drowning those frustrations in a mid-afternoon movie or other diversion. It's not a terrible thing to do—it can even help at times—unless it becomes a habit.

When they begin a new project, Weeks and Abbott make a formal start. They set up a notebook with ideas and plans and discuss the project together before retiring to their separate work rooms. Organization and discipline are important, Sarah says, but that's not the whole story. She feels that when she has a good idea for a lyric, it all comes together quite quickly. When she struggles and agonizes over each word, she finds that the end product is often not as good.

Michael agrees that this is an inexplicable part of "the creative process." There is an element of inspiration without which all the training and experience one may have are not enough. Even the most terrific idea requires careful working out; it must be developed, expanded, refined—transformed from a bit of inspiration into a complete song. Yet inspiration, as the word itself denotes, is the breath of life of any creative endeavor.

You may be filled with inspiration, and even write wonderful songs, without achieving success or recognition. It's hard to calculate how many aspiring songwriters there are in this country, so that to make an estimate of their success rate is difficult. However, when I asked Weeks and Abbott how many songwriters in a thousand actually "make it," Sarah thought for a moment and said, "Three." Michael thought that was a fairly accurate estimate.

Writing songs for yourself or others is a terrifically competitive field. There are, however, some ways in which songwriters can gain experience and make important connections in the field. Both Sarah and Michael feel they owe much of their current success to a workshop sponsored by ASCAP, the American Society of Composers, Authors and Publishers. The ASCAP workshop, in turn, led to their participation in the Mentor Program of the Dramatists Guild.

ASCAP functions as a royalty-collecting agency for composers. The organization monitors all performances (live and broadcast) of the works of its members and collects royalties, which are split between ASCAP and the composer. It is in ASCAP's interest to attract new composers to its ranks as a potential source of royalty money. For this reason, it sponsors free workshops in songwriting, open by audition, into which Weeks and Abbott were accepted as a team.

The ASCAP workshop gave both lyricist and composer new insights into their technique. It also allowed them to observe the work of their colleagues firsthand. Perhaps most important, ASCAP announced a joint program with the Dramatists Guild (an organization that serves a similar function for playwrights and lyricists) in which a limited number of songwriters would have the opportunity to work closely with a mentor, an established composer or lyricist who would give them individual help as well as an entree into the professional world.

Weeks and Abbott were accepted into this program and began to work with a famous songwriter who has a number of Broadway shows to his credit. He recommended them to the people at "Sesame Street." Through the Mentor Program, they met other writers and composers. One, a successful playwright, introduced them to his agent, who signed them on. These connections have been invaluable, not only in establishing the professional credibility of Weeks and Abbott, but also in opening doors that might otherwise have been closed to them.

Songwriting is no exception in the music world—connections, and your ability to function socially as well as professionally, are extremely important. There are added logistical problems for songwriters. If you want to make this your career, you had better plan to settle in New York. Just as with commercial music performance, Los Angeles is a possibility, particularly if writing for the movies is your interest, but there is really no other choice of locale.

Being in one of these big cities is also important because it puts you in the mainstream of the music that is currently being written and performed, as well as providing access to the history of American songwriting. Sarah and Michael have steeped themselves in the music of our great popular composers and lyricists: Gershwin, Bernstein, Sondheim, Yip Harburg, Randy Newman, Paul Simon—and performers: Bill Evans, Art Tatum, and others. In addition, they keep abreast of what is going on in the clubs, on the radio, and in the record industry. In New York, all of this is at your fingertips—record stores for new and vintage recordings, the Library of the Performing Arts with its impressive record collection and archives, numerous clubs, and radio stations of all kinds. The big cities are also filled with people whose knowledge of American popular music is enormous. If you want to make it in this field, you too must become an expert in the genre.

When I finished talking with Sarah and Michael, I left feeling that they had passed along to me the sense of hopeful realism they have about their joint careers. They have a mutually supportive relationship, and I think they both see this as an asset to their individual and shared success. Although they both say they would be open to pursuing separate projects, even if it meant being apart for a time, they definitely see themselves as a team for the long run. Obviously, not every songwriting team will be a husband and wife team, and in some instances that kind of proximity could be detrimental. Yet it does help Sarah and Michael to avoid some of the problems couples face when one or both are involved in demanding, more than full-time, careers.

Professionally, they are deservedly proud of their achievements, without seeing them as a guarantee of a successful future. There are no real guarantees in this profession unless perhaps you reach the quasi-legendary status of the "greats." Yet even a Stephen Sondheim can get a bad review. Styles change, influences change, inspiration, luck, and concentration wax and wane.

The bottom line is a great deal of talent. Discipline, perseverance, ability to hustle, to make connections, to be in the right place at the right time all build on that basis of talent. If the music and the words are in you and you're burning to let them out, become your own best critic. Learn about popular music, listen to what's going on around you, assess your talent and commitment in terms of what's gone before and what's likely to be ahead. If you think you've got "the right stuff," give it your all and more. Anything less won't be enough.

Chapter **VI**

Careers in Performing, Composing and Conducting

I consulted Webster's Dictionary for some inspiration to begin our exploration of performing careers in classical music. Sometimes the dictionary definition of a word sheds new light on its many connotations and shades of meaning. Yet, in the case of "perform," "performance," and like words, I was sorely disappointed. "To carry out...to present in a manner following prescribed procedure ...to accomplish..." were about the extent of the definitions offered. Yes, I thought to myself, performance is certainly all of those things, but it is so much more. Performance has a power that attracts, drives, and sustains musicians to work like fiends and then plunge themselves into an extraordinarily competitive environment. Great performances can bring about emotional epiphanies and can remain etched in the memory of the onlooker for years to come.

Perhaps the only way to do justice to the art of performing is to explore it in terms of various performing careers. In this section we will discuss instrumentalists, singers, and conductors. We'll look at free-lance players, chorus members, and soloists of all kinds. You may begin to get an idea of the many external factors involved in having a career in performance. Equally important, you will discover some of the *internal* factors—qualities you will need to possess and nurture in yourself if you truly wish to be a performing artist.

How does one decide on a career in the performing arts? Just think about the millions of American school kids who are handed band or orchestra instruments in about fourth grade or so. They take lessons in school, play with a group, and practice—more or less diligently. Out of that common experience, which so many of us have shared, how do our future performers develop? Talent helps, but at the beginning stages your interest in and enthusiasm for music are probably just as important. Any observant teacher will clue into an unusual degree of curiosity and desire to learn on the part of a student. A teacher will be able to enrich a student's musical education, expand his or her musical horizons. At the same time, your initial interest in music will be only the very beginning of your own process of self-education, your self-motivated pursuit of excellence.

You have to love to perform if you are going to consider performing professionally. Many talented players and singers have an absolute dread of walking on stage. Theirs is not ordinary stage fright, but a paralyzing fear of being in front of an audience. Such people are ill suited to performance, even though they may be original and sensitive interpreters and masterful technicians in the privacy of their own homes. In a very few cases, musicians have built careers almost exclusively through recordings, but those tend to be lopsided careers. The public craves the rare appearances of these elusive artists, because the essence of performance is *live* performance. Performance is a partnership between artist and audience. The performer opens himself or herself to the audience; and the audience, in turn, must allow itself to be carried along by the force of the performer's art.

The decision to seek a performing career may take you by surprise. That is, it may seem less like a decision than a foregone conclusion. As music itself becomes more and more compelling to you, music-making will become more and more the focus of your life. You will devote yourself to your music perhaps without even declaring consciously to yourself that there is nothing else you could or would want to be doing with your life. Of course, every aspiring performer has a moment of realizing how important music is to him or her. You will recognize that a great piece of music expresses, in a certain sense, all of the accumulated wisdom and emotion of the world in a brief span of time. Nothing can be more important than your being able to express that wisdom and that emotion, through the music, as a performing artist.

That sounds like very powerful stuff, and it is. A performing career requires fierce commitment and demands great sacrifices, personal and material. If you can accept the need for these sacrifices on your part, you may get the chance to experience the rewards of performance. Performance can be exhilarating and fulfilling in the strongest sense of the word. It takes a certain kind of courage to pursue a career in performance. Let's explore this more closely as we look at various performing careers in classical music.

ORCHESTRAL PLAYING

If you are an instrumentalist and have had the opportunity to play in an orchestra or a band, you have probably experienced the tremendous excitement generated by a large ensemble working together toward a single musical goal. Even if you have not had the chance to play in a group, you may have heard great performances by an orchestra on a nationwide tour or by a professional orchestra based in your area.

Most instrumentalists aiming for a performing career in classical music aspire to be orchestral players. This is not only because there is more opportunity in this field than in solo playing or chamber music, but also because orchestral playing can be so rewarding—personally, artistically, and financially.

Professional orchestral playing in America provides full-time—or at least steady part-time—employment for the small but increasing number of players who are orchestral members. These increasing numbers are attributable to the fact that new and viable ensembles are currently establishing themselves throughout the country. The two coasts and the major Midwestern cities no longer exercise a monopoly over professional orchestral music. The American Federation of Musicians, the largest union of musicians in this country, states that there are some thirty-four major symphony orchestras in the United States and Canada today.

An orchestral job has three major requirements, interrelated and equally important. They are: expertise on your particular instrument, knowledge of the repertoire, and ensemble ability. The first requirement may be the most obvious. The first impression you will make at an orchestral audition is how well you play: tone quality, intonation, breath support or bow control, agility, ability to shape a phrase, overall musicality. If you do not play well, you won't have the opportunity to show your strength in other areas. We live in a musical age in which accurate technique is stressed and in which many people achieve an impressive degree of technical mastery of their instruments. Technical expertise is an essential step, but it is only the first step.

Courtesy the New York Philharmonic

The New York Philharmonic in Avery Fisher Hall.

Familiarity with the orchestral repertoire is required of all orchestral players, because one will often perform a concert after only one or two rehearsals. Compare this to the weeks, or even months, that you have spent rehearsing in school or community orchestras and bands, and then think of the quality of presentation of a major symphony orchestra. Their concerts are by no means thrown together, nor are the rehearsals merely an attempt to "put a piece together." Rather, the individual players come into rehearsal so well prepared, and with the knowledge that there is such a limited amount of time to achieve a quality performance, that they are able to concentrate their work and produce results that lesser players would need far more time to achieve.

Knowledge of the repertoire will also help you to develop your ensemble abilities. Good ensemble playing, simply put, is the ability to perform your particular part *in the context* not only of other instruments' particular parts, but also of the piece as a whole. If you are a violinist, you must master your part, but you must also know when the flute has a passage of particular importance so that you can adjust your playing accordingly. If you have a long rest in the middle of a piece, you must be aware of changes in tempo and key that are occurring around you, so that when you begin to play again, you do so in the context of the changes that have occurred.

It is true that a conductor gives you many specific directions to help ensemble playing. After all, it is the ensemble as a whole that is a conductor's instrument, and a conductor's interpretation will shape the context of the music you play. Yet a conductor will not be able to "play" his or her instrument if that instrument is not well tuned and prepared. That "tuning" is each player's attention to his or her own part *and* to the other parts of a piece. It is also the ability to make intelligent musical decisions, based on a knowledge of the ensemble as a whole, as to how one's own part should be played.

Ensemble ability can be developed and improved by teaching and practicing. However, you must have within yourself, initially, a sensitivity to and respect for the demands of ensemble playing. This is something each person must discover and cultivate. You may discover it listening to a great performance or having a good experience in an ensemble yourself. This sensitivity and respect, in combination with good preparation and abilities in the other areas mentioned above, will allow you to adapt yourself successfully to many kinds of ensemble playing, from a baroque concerto grosso to a late Romantic symphony to a twentieth-century work or an oratorio with choir and soloists.

Competitive auditions before a committee made up of the conductor and other players determine who will gain a spot in a professional symphony orchestra. Such auditions are advertised in music journals and newsletters, through conservatories, at summer music festivals, and by word of mouth. An initial secreening of applications may weed out some candidates, but it is not unusual for the audition committee to hear one hundred or more players competing for a single position in the preliminary round.

At most auditions today, the player is hidden from the committee by a screen. The player's identity is not revealed and there is no discussion beforehand, so that the first and only impression the committee receives is the sound the player produces. This system was devised to protect both player and committee from partiality; neither favorable nor unfavorable circumstances should influence the purely aural judgment of the committee.

If you are accepted at the level of the preliminary auditions, you will have at least two more rounds to go before a final decision is made. At each level, the committee will judge your ability in the solo repertoire, in purely technical exercises, and in orchestral excerpts.

To have a successful audition, you must be able to prove yourself to the committee in all three areas discussed above: technical expertise, knowledge of the repertoire, and ensemble playing. The first, "blind" impression you make will be based in great part on technical expertise. Even at this level, however, the other two elements come into play. Later rounds of your audition may include actually playing as part of an ensemble, but, even behind a screen and playing alone, you will have to communicate your abilities as an ensemble player in the orchestral excerpts you play.

You must be thoroughly familiar with all of the orchestral repertoire you may be asked to play. The knowledge of the repertoire that we discussed earlier cannot be achieved *after* you become a member of a professional orchestra. That knowledge is an essential part of your preparation for an audition, and it is preparation that may have to be done largely on your own. Although, as the field gets more competitive, many orchestras prefer to consider candidates with prior professional experience, some players may go into auditions with only school orchestral experience behind them. They may never have had the opportunity to play a certain excerpt in context before they are called upon to play it at an audition. If that is the case, the player should take the initiative to study the score and listen to several recordings of the work, to gain an understanding not only of one's own part, but of the piece as a whole.

☆   ☆   ☆

The major symphony orchestras, which provide full-time employment, typically require eight "services" per week of their members. These "services" break down to four rehearsals and four performances. Recording sessions and other special events such as television broadcasts are extra service and are compensated accordingly. The orchestra's season may include concerts in its home city and tours here and abroad, for which the players receive a per diem (daily allowance) for living expenses in addition to their salaries. Salaries for the major orchestras average between $20,000 and $25,000 per year.

Full-time orchestral members receive approximately four weeks of paid vacation each year. In many cases they have the option of taking off several more weeks without pay. This vacation time is not as flexible as in many other jobs, but is determined by the orchestra's season. Many orchestras participate in summer festivals, but most do break for at least part of the summer, which is when their members take their vacations.

The part-time orchestral playing referred to above is not primarily free-lance work, that is, the kind of ensemble that comes together for one concert or series of concerts. We'll look at freelance playing in a separate section later on in this chapter. Rather, there are orchestras with shorter seasons or fewer concerts than the major symphony orchestras, but which are permanent, ongoing groups nonetheless. These orchestras tend to base themselves in one locale and serve the needs of the immediate community. They may even perform a number of functions, not only presenting symphony concerts, but perhaps playing for a touring ballet or opera company. In major cities the opera and ballet companies have their own orchestras. You may want to explore a position with one of those orchestras. This is a somewhat different experience than symphony orchestra playing: the repertoire is different, and the orchestra, playing from the pit, forms only one part of a whole evening of musical drama, rather than its sole focus.

Players with part-time orchestral employment will certainly have to seek ways to supplement their income. Full-time players who are single or without dependents will probably find their salary sufficient. However, those who have families or large expenses may find that they must also take on other work.

Teaching is a common source of income for orchestral players. Many are associated with colleges or conservatories, although this is not essential. For some players, teaching actually becomes a second full-time career. Students are eager to study with teachers who themselves have successful performing careers; a performing teacher's limited free hours are often in great demand.

Fitting a teaching schedule into an already busy schedule of rehearsals and concerts can be tricky, and it puts a lot of extra pressure on a player. On a day when there is a rehearsal in the morning and a concert in the evening, a player might have to spend the afternoon teaching rather than resting and preparing for the evening's performance.

The dual career of performer and teacher is quite common in the music world, but it does pose a number of problems, apart from schedule difficulties, for the musician and his or her students. If you study with someone like this, you may have run into some of these problems. You will certainly encounter them if you yourself perform and teach some day.

The problems center around the sometimes conflicting needs of teacher and student. As a student, you know that it is important for you to have a consistent schedule of study and practice. You probably like to see your teacher on a weekly schedule, knowing that you could also consult him or her if special circumstances arose. If you are lucky, your relationship with your teacher goes beyond the imparting and receiving of technical information. Your teacher may take part in your development not only as a player, but as a musician and a person as a whole. The two of you may share the excitement of working toward the goal of ever better music-making.

If you become a teacher, it is to be hoped that you will strive for full relationships with your students. Consistency is perhaps as important for you as for your students, in order to keep abreast of their problems and progress. At the same time, if you are a performer, the mere fact of your performing schedule may prevent you from seeing each of your students on a weekly basis. When you are on tour, you won't see your students for long periods of time. Even when you are at home, you must allow time for your own study and practice.

Allowing time for your own work may be the most difficult but also the most important thing a teacher/performer does. Of course, if you have a successful solo career, there is no question that your own practice will be a priority, and your relationships with your students will be limited accordingly. If, however, you are an orchestral player, already familiar with all or most of the repertoire you are required to play, there may be a temptation simply to try to maintain a certain level of proficiency, rather than to continue growing and improving. If you need to teach a lot for economic reasons you may not have enough time to practice, even if the inclination exists. In the long run, however, the attitude of "maintenance" practice will almost certainly cause a decline in your level of accomplishment. Teaching others may help to shed light on your own strengths and weaknesses as a player, but it is not a substitute for attacking your own technique and musicianship directly. Moreover, practice is an important way for a teacher to gain insight into students' particular needs and problems. If you are teaching a student who encounters a difficulty you cannot immediately solve, you may have to physicalize the problem for yourself, in your own practice, in order to understand it more fully.

The problems and rewards of juggling a teaching career and a performing career are only part of the many elements that go into a successful orchestral playing career. To return to the beginning of such a career, one question I asked of professional orchestral players that provided many interesting responses was, "How did you know you were ready to audition for your job?" The answer was invariably that they didn't know. In fact, many were convinced that they didn't have the slightest chance of getting the job. No one could provide me with a magic formula to answer my question; no magic formula exists. But the question did lead to informative discussions of the kind of preparation that *did* lead to a successful audition.

"Preparation," I found out, means not only the work you will do for a specific audition, but the whole way you have educated yourself musically, and even aspects of your life-style that may help you as a musician. We have discussed the technical, repertoire, and ensemble requirements you will need for an orchestral job. In a sense, you have been preparing these skills since you began studying music. However, it is at a college or conservatory that you can begin to expand these skills and to hone in on the specific area of music in which you will concentrate.

A college or conservatory offers several advantages for this kind of skill building. You will probably hear more music and more different kinds of music than you ever have before. Most conservatories or schools with strong music departments have orchestras, bands, choirs, chamber ensembles, jazz ensembles, contemporary music ensembles, and groups specializing in early music and even non-Western music. Many schools have concert series bringing in great performers from outside and recitals by students and faculty members. You should take advantage of as many performances, rehearsals, and master classes as possible, even in areas unrelated to your particular interest. You may discover an even greater interest in some area of music with which you were previously unfamiliar. At the very least, you will expand your musical vocabulary, making your own musical expression that much richer.

A listening library is another great resource of a college or conservatory. The combination of good stereo equipment, recordings, and scores, so that you can follow what you are hearing, makes a wonderful tool, and you should take full advantage of it. The listening library is the place to learn the repertoire that you may someday have to play at short notice. With the score in hand, you can get not only an overview, but detailed knowledge about a piece.

A listening room allows you to compare performances and to hear great performances of the past. Comparative listening is extremely important for the development of that elusive quality "style," the collective body of ideas and traditions about how a piece of music should sound. This is not to say that you should listen to a great performance and try to copy it note for note. That will not help you achieve the proper "style," because any one performance is always a mixture of accepted wisdom and purely individual conviction—good and bad. Listening to different performances should provide you with a strong foundation upon which you will build your own interpretation and sense of style.

Apart from listening, performing, and practicing, you should make a thorough check of the academic courses available at your school. The musicians with whom I spoke found music theory and ear training important and useful tools in their work. Consider history courses and courses dealing with the literature of instruments other than your own. Flute players have told me how much they have learned from the vocal repertoire; pianists, from string chamber music.

Your own curiosity and your willingness to explore the things about which you are curious can make the difference between being an adequate musician and an excellent musician. Many players, particularly wind players, have begun to explore breathing and alignment disciplines, such as yoga, tai-chi, or Alexander technique. These nonmusical activities can and do have a direct impact on your playing, making you more aware of the source of your energies and thus more able to direct them to your playing. Some musicians take this physical awareness even further and pay strict attention to diet and nutrition. Of course, these outside disciplines are not for everyone, and it would be wrong to imply that skill in yoga or a certain kind of diet will result in a successful orchestra audition. However, in the competitive world of professional orchestra playing, many, many elements are required for success. It is up to you to discover and develop the things that will make you the finest musician you can be.

CHAMBER MUSIC

If you are a reader of the arts section of any national newspaper or magazine, chances are you will have read an article on a subject that is extremely fashionable today: the current boom in American chamber music. "Boom" is probably the last word I would use in the context of chamber music, and the story is more complicated than that word might lead us to believe. Yet it is true that there is strong interest in and growing opportunities for the performance of chamber music by established and new groups in America today. The field is narrow and extremely competitive. Perhaps one in ten *professional* chamber ensembles will have the success and longevity to provide its members with steady careers. The work and its life-style are arduous. But for some musicians, no other kind of music provides the challenge or inspires the dedication that chamber music does. If you are such a musician, this section may help you in your pursuit of a career in chamber music.

What is chamber music? Quite literally, it is music to be performed in a chamber, that is, a small, intimate space. Historically, much chamber music was composed for patron, friends, or family members; composers intended this music for at-home music-making and entertainment rather than for public spectacle.

Much has changed since the days when every educated person was expected to be a competent musician. The family that gathers for an evening of chamber music today is far more likely to go to a concert hall than to set up instruments, stands, and scores in their own living room. Not only are our definitions of performer and audience different today; we have also redefined our ideas of the proper forum for hearing great music.

And chamber music *is* great music. Listen to a recording of a Schubert quartet and think about a funny-looking little man and his music-making friends who got together for chamber music evenings they called Schubertiads. They weren't reading through trifles, but through some of the most sublime music ever written. Today our attitude toward great music is that it should not be restricted to its "chamber." It should be performed publicly for as wide an audience as possible. Chamber music is an intimate art form with mass appeal. Striking a balance between those two elements is a task confronting today's chamber musicians.

The term "chamber music" is used very broadly and often as a catch-all classification for otherwise hard-to-classify music. I prefer a fairly narrow definition of chamber music in the professional sense. There are criteria for a *career* in chamber music that I believe define and restrict the repertoire. One criterion is that the dynamic of a chamber ensemble and its music be what I think of as democratic. Chamber music is not, essentially, the music of a soloist and accompanists, or leaders and followers, but of separate but equal voices. In today's music world, I believe, this criterion effectively rules out the sonata repertoire and the voice/piano literature as chamber music. That is because of our tendency to view such music as soloistic, as we will discuss in the next section, on collaborative pianists.

Another criterion is that a career in chamber music requires *at least* a full-time commitment to chamber music. A professional quartet player cannot also pursue a solo career or play in an orchestra. A soloist may make occasional, or even frequent, appearances in chamber concerts, but he or she appears as guest, not as a career chamber musician.

In terms of repertoire, this means that there are many works of "chamber music" that are rarely, if ever, performed by an ongoing ensemble, but rather by an ensemble and guest or guests. Logistics usually dictate that rehearsal of such works be restricted to a bare minimum. Guest artists can rarely achieve that rapport of the regular ensemble with one another or with their particular performing style. This does not mean that nothing can be called chamber music that does not meet these criteria. Indeed, it is just these works for unusual combinations that should be explored by musicians in their own homes, the original forum of chamber music, for their own pleasure if nothing else. The mainstay of a professional ensemble's repertoire must be, however, the music they continually practice and perform as a unit. It is with this repertoire that they will achieve that greatest level of artistry and make true "chamber music."

This artistry has to do with an ideal of *ensemble* playing for which groups strive and which audiences find very exciting. The members of a great quartet often seem to move and breathe as if they were physically connected to one another. Their bodies manifest their ideas about the music—that it should sound as one voice. This striving for ensemble creates a powerful dynamic in great chamber music performances.

The music that fulfills these criteria is the rich repertoire of string, woodwind, and brass trios, quartets, quintets, and various other groupings. String quartets are by far the most visible and numerous kind of chamber ensembles. In general, there is more opportunity in professional chamber music for string players than for brass, woodwinds, or pianists. There is more string repertoire of a greater variety than exists for the other instruments. Contemporary composers may move beyond these traditional groupings, but theirs is a limited output with a limited audience.

How do you get to play this wonderful music professionally? You've got to be talented and well advanced technically and musically, even at a young age. You've got to work extremely hard —more on that later. And, to be quite honest, you've got to have very good luck.

These are three key elements in the chamber music mix, although they may not seem very clear-cut or even fair. I know players with a serious love for and commitment to chamber music who simply started too late to be able to make a serious attempt at a career. Others find the day-in, day-out, year-round rehearsal too taxing, or are unable to make ends meet in the tough initial years when engagements are few and far between.

The element of luck is probably the trickiest to pin down. Some of it is "being in the right place at the right time" luck. Many chamber musicians with whom I've spoken feel that urban living was crucial to their development—specifically, the opportunity to study and work in a major cultural center. Yet not every music student can attend school in a big city, at least not at the undergraduate level.

Knowing the "right" people is another part of one's musical luck. Today many successful American chamber musicians can trace their success back to their association with members of the Juilliard String Quartet. The Cleveland Quartet, in residence at the Eastman School of Music in Rochester, New York, has initiated a program that is helping to train a new generation of professional chamber musicians.

One chamber musician I know, who began working with the Juilliard Quartet at the age of twenty, describes them quite unequivocally as his mentors. He characterizes his years at Juilliard—undergraduate, graduate, and in Professional Studies—as being in "a womb" of work, study, and the nurturing of his talents. Young chamber musicians should seek out such mentors, and stay in "the womb" as long as possible, he says, gaining the expertise they will need in the professional world without the pressures of that world. The desire to enter"real life" may be a misguided one for young chamber musicians. If you are lucky enough to have mentors, you may want to prolong your student years until you are good enough and experienced enough to compete successfully as a professional.

The American String Quartet.   *Photo: Jack Mitchell*

When you are ready to leave school, what do you do? At this point, another element of luck comes into play. A sure way for a young ensemble to make itself known is to win a major chamber music competition. In America, the two most prestigious of these are the Naumburg Competition in New York and the Coleman Competition in California. The American String Quartet, one of the most successful young quartets performing today, won both of these competitions in a single year. These successes provided them with their first engagements and made them known not only to the music-loving public, but to managements, one of which signed them on.

Winning competitions, however, is a tricky business, and as I implied in the last paragraph, not a little luck is involved. It is not necessarily a measure of your talent or potential for success. Some people are simply not "competition people." If you are not, discovering that by doing poorly in one or more competitions can be a devastating experience. Even if you do compete well, merit is simply one element of your success. Subtle factors such as the playing style of your ensemble or the repertoire you choose will affect the outcome. I can't deny, also, that the element of "politics" may come into play. Judges and performers are only human, and it would be unrealistic to think that a competition could be free of all influences but the sounds of the music.

If your ensemble does win a chamber music competition, several doors may open to you. As in the case of the American String Quartet, a management may take you on, arranging for engagements and other aspects of your professional life such as publicity and travel. However, even if this does not come about, your ensemble may be able to promote itself quite successfully. The American Quartet left their management after a few years and did not immediately sign with anyone else. On their own, they developed a publicity packet and a basic contract. They then consulted *Musical America*, the "must have" encyclopedic guide to music and musicians in this country, and made up a mailing list of all suitable chamber music series in America. The quartet contacted the people who booked these series, negotiated their own fees, and made all of their own travel and other arrangements. This situation worked well for them when their season averaged twenty-five performances. Not only were they not obligated to pay a manager's commission, but they gained invaluable knowledge of the mechanics of the music business.

A resource that was not available to the American String Quartet is the recently established Chamber Music America. This organization, based in New York, serves as a clearinghouse for young professional chamber ensembles. Founded in 1977, Chamber Music America (CMA), according to its executive director, "grew out of the needs of performing groups themselves. We didn't know how to get management, whether to incorporate, how to get grants, or start our own subscription series.'' CMA gives individual consultation, referrals, and advice to its members. It publishes *American Ensemble* quarterly, a publication specifically geared to current events in the world of chamber music. CMA compiles directories of information helpful to young chamber music groups and can also do individualized funding searches. It sponsors semiannual conferences, makes helpful publications available at cost, distributes mailing lists, and offers major medical insurance to its members, who pay annual dues based on a percentage of their performing income. Not only performing groups become members of CMA, but also those who present chamber music concerts as well as chamber music training programs. Nonvoting members can include interested amateurs, students, and individuals. CMA's Board of Directors and Advisory Council include some of America's most successful chamber musicians, such as Robert Mann of the Juilliard String Quartet, Robert Biddlecome of the American Brass Quintet, and the singer Jan DeGaetani.

The young ensemble able to put together twenty-five engagements per year must be well on the way to success, but it won't make ends meet. Individually or collectively, the ensemble must have another souce of income. Some players turn to free-lance work, which we will explore in depth in a later section. Chamber musicians often have success at free-lance playing, because if they are good enough to be professional chamber musicians, they are certainly qualified and well connected enough to be hired by free-lance contractors. Free-lance work, however, is a viable alternative only in a few cities: New York, Los Angeles, perhaps Chicago, Boston, and San Francisco. This may change as other cities expand their cultural life. At present, however, the situation limits you to a very few locales.

The most constructive source of other income for a quartet, even if their career is well established, is a residency at a music school or university. Residencies combine individual teaching, ensemble teaching, coaching, and performing. Not only do they provide an important respite from traveling, but most ensembles feel that teaching enriches their own artistry and they value their teaching time highly.

In the past it was considered desirable, if not necessary, to secure a residency in a large city, for the reason of being in the thick of a thriving musical life. Now, for various reasons, ensembles are advised to accept residencies in more isolated locations. Competition makes this necessary. More and better ensembles than ever compete for a limited number of residencies: an ensemble is lucky to get any position at all. Smaller or more isolated institutions are not necessarily less well equipped to support excellent chamber music programs. One player told me that he enjoyed one of the greatest performing experiences of his life in a nearly perfect chamber music hall on the campus of the University of Kansas at Lawrence.

Residencies, wherever they may be, provide a great impetus for a young ensemble to learn and perfect repertoire. If you are contracted to give four concerts per year at your school, not only will you have to prepare four completely distinct programs, but you will have the added pressure of performing for an audience of your colleagues and students. This is a kind of trial by fire that can prepare an ensemble for the most demanding performing situations.

A residency is likely to be an important part of the professional chamber music life-style, whether you have 25 or 125 engagements per season; and the more successful groups do have that many engagements—an average of a concert every two or three days. Travel thus becomes a way of life for chamber musicians. Some groups actually travel to their "residencies," if their time commitment there is limited and they choose to live elsewhere. *All* groups must travel to perform. Travel can be interesting and fun, or inconvenient and exhausting. It is definitely expensive and often time-consuming. The amount of travel required of chamber musicians affects every part of their lives: relationships with family and friends, type of home base and attitude toward that home, and so on. Some musicians (particularly those with the most unwieldy instruments!) become active members of travelers' associations and work to improve conditions on the modes of travel they must use so often. Many musicians agree that the constant traveling they must do is far more difficult than their actual performance obligations.

If travel is one pole that orients chamber music life, practice may be the other. There is no way to get around the fact that all ensembles must work long and hard to achieve the excitement of a cohesive chamber music performance, which can be overwhelming, but so often elusive. Every detail of dynamics, tempo, phrasing, and style, as well as the overall scope of each piece, must be worked out among the separate and occasionally divergent musical personalities of the ensemble members. There is always new repertoire to learn, and old repertoire must be maintained and improved upon. Six and even seven days per week, four hours per day, all year long—this is a not uncommon practice regimen for professional chamber musicians. The best established ensembles may take the luxury of summers off, but most groups cannot afford to do this.

Traveling and practicing with the members of your ensemble entails more than getting from one place to another and putting together the parts of a piece of music. These are people with whom you spend by far most of your time, working, performing, and socializing. The relationships among ensemble members clearly extend beyond the purely professional. Something as fundamental as where you live will probably be determined by where other members of the ensemble live, because you must have easy access to each other for rehearsals. Traveling, which can be a lonely experience, may tend to bring ensemble members together for socializing as well as working.

In daily practice, the hashing out of musical questions involves not only your professional expertise, but all aspects of your personality, mood, state of mind, for better or worse. The stakes are high, because the standards are so high. Chamber music may be "democratic," but more specifically, it is the democracy of soloists. Each ensemble member must hold up his or her own end and assert the importance of his or her part. The members of your ensemble may be your staunchest allies, or they may get on your nerves. In either case, the intensity of relationships within an ensemble is an important aspect of the chamber music life-style.

Occasionally the interrelationships of members of an ensemble do not work out, and a painful but necessary change of personnel is called for. Often an ensemble forms simply because its members find they are compatible music-makers, on a similar level of development and able to work well together. They may not know each other well personally, nor may they have a clue as to the others' values and ideas on other than musical questions. When these larger issues come into play, ensembles may find that there are irreconcilable differences among them. This is a caution to those of you who are looking to form chamber music ensembles. Get to know your fellow players' ideas, not only on style in Mozart quartets, but on the size of the career you aspire to have, where you want to live, how you want to organize your practice schedule. Consider that these are people with whom you will work in the closest way for years and years to come.

I don't want to leave the topic of life-style without discussing the economics of professional chamber music. I have talked about residencies and even free-lance playing as bread-and-butter supplements to performing income. At the same time, chamber music has quite a glamorous reputation—travel, engagements in prestigious halls, successful recordings. Where does the financial truth lie? A member of the American String Quarter put it to me quite precisely. "Last year," he said, "my unadjusted gross income was $33,000." "Not bad," I thought to myself, until he added, "my adjusted gross was $3,500."

What does this mean? The $33,000 figure refers to a salary for the quartet's residency at the Peabody Conservatory in Baltimore, plus a share of the fees received for concerts. The $3,500 figure refers to what was left after travel expenses, management and promotional fees, instrument maintenance, and other professional expenditures were paid out. Now, as a self-employed person, a chamber musician can claim many living expenses as professional expenses, including portions of rent and entertainment, so that the $3,500 figure does not describe all the money my friend had to live on last year. Still, it is not a lot of money, particularly by big-city standards.

Even a quartet that has been around longer and has issued several successful recordings may make less money that you would think. In an interview that appeared several years ago in the *New York Times Magazine,* members of the Cleveland Quartet estimated that they earned approximately $20,000 a year after expenses. It seems surprising that the quartet's recodings did not improve their financial situation greatly. Yet today, making a recording, even a successful one, does not mean instant wealth from royalty payments. The expenses of producing and promoting a recording must be recovered. In addition, securing a recording contract may require a substantial outside investment. Record companies may not otherwise risk working with a group. The days are gone when brilliant young musicians were discovered and handed lucrative recording contracts. Today's brilliant musicians know where and how to go about raising money to back their initial recordings.

Working in chamber music is a labor of love. Advantages of solo and ensemble playing accrue to chamber music: you are a soloist within an extremely tight ensemble. In this competitive and exciting field, success may ride in no small part upon your ability to work closely and well with your fellow ensemble members, through long hours of practicing, promoting, traveling, and performing. Consider well not only your musical partners, but your strengths and weaknesses in relating personally and artistically to others. Chamber musicians must achieve a high level of communication among themselves before they put their wonderful music to work as a communicative tool between ensemble and audience.

COLLABORATIVE PIANISTS

One professional choice that exists for pianists is that of performing in collaboration with other musicians—instrumentalists or singers, soloists or chamber ensembles. You may be accustomed to calling such pianists "accompanists." I prefer the term "collaborator." It implies an equality of participation and musical input and output that is essential to a great performance.

The fact that the issue of names even arises attests to some of the peculiar complexities of this profession. Gerald Moore, one of the most renowned collaborative pianists of this century, wrote several books about his profession. With titles such as *The Unashamed Accompanist* and *Am I Too Loud?*, you can see that even the finest pianists have found ideal "collaboration" difficult to achieve.

Collaboration—ideal or otherwise—means rehearsing and performing the repertoire written for piano and one or more voices or instruments. In some cases, a pianist has a permanent association with a chamber ensemble or a small vocal ensemble. Other pianists are independent, in the sense that they work with many artists and are hired per engagement. Although such pianists may do most of their performing with only a very few artists, it is highly unusual for a pianist and an instrumentalist or a singer to develop an exclusive or formal association, as a chamber ensemble does. Exceptions to this have been some family performing teams—husband-wife or brother-sister collaborations. Superstars such as Jascha Heifetz have had exclusive arrangements with pianists. On the more usual per-engagement basis, there are no regular or fixed rehearsals. Most performances must come together on a minimum of rehearsal time, often squeezed into the busy and independent schedules of pianist and soloist.

Most collaborative pianists work with both instrumentalists and singers, simply because, in a highly competitive field, such versatility is necessary. If they work with singers at all, they probably assume the additional role of vocal coach, another hard-to-define but extremely important profession.

A coach helps a singer to prepare for a performance or audition. The kind of ''help'' this entails depends on the persons involved. Some singers may have trouble mastering notes and rhythms, particularly in conjunction with a complicated accompaniment. A coach must be familiar enough with the voice *and* piano parts of any piece to be able to help singers not only with their line, but with the relationship between the parts.

Many singers seek out a coach for help with diction; that is, the often difficult task of pronouncing words clearly while singing beautifully. Diction presents problems particularly if a singer must perform in a language he or she does not speak. At the very least, a coach must have a thorough knowledge of the pronunciation of several foreign languages as well as an understanding of the grammar and structure of those languages. One is necessary to help a singer achieve an authentic sound. The other is essential to forming a convincing interpretation. Singers performing in an unfamiliar language must have a word-for-word translation of the text. If they don't know the meaning of each word they sing, they will never be able to communicate effectively with an audience. A coach may be the only person they can turn to for help with making a translation.

Coaches can also help singers with the fine points of style of the different kinds of music they may have to perform. A singer with an active career may be involved in opera, oratorio, and recital music of all periods. Stylistic insights that a coach can offer may be of help in interpreting the music.

I emphasize the *help* that coaches offer in all of these areas, as opposed to a situation in which a coach does everything for the singer (short of actually singing!), including providing a ready-made interpretation that the singer merely learns by rote. Remember that *collaboration* is the key word. Singer and coach must discuss every aspect of a performance, exchanging knowledge and ideas. A coach must know how to point a singer in the right direction without dictating the shape of every note and phrase. Of course, this is as much the responsibility of the singer as it is of the pianist.

In all of this discussion, I've talked very little about the piano, per se. This is one of the pitfalls for pianists who do most of their work with others; the importance and extent of their individual talents may be pushed into the background. In many cases, a pianist will be playing a part that was not even written specifically for piano, but is an orchestral reduction or a harpsichord part. It takes great expertise to make reductions approximate the sound of a full orchestra or to make a piano sound like a harpsichord, but this expertise may be little appreciated, and the part will almost certainly not be pianistically grateful to play.

Many "soloists"—singers and instrumentalists—think everything is fine if their "accompanist" simply plays all the notes in the right rhythm, "keeps the beat going," "provides a good solid background." Some may insist that their interpretations are inviolable, meaning that they close themselves off to any exchange of ideas and expect the pianist simply to follow their ideas. This is the kind of attitude that makes for frustrated pianists *and* performances that are less good than they could be.

A far better attitude for performers and performance exists if the coach/pianist is able to express himself or herself more fully as a *pianist*. "Soloists" will find that they understand a piece far better if they appreciate the richness and importance of what the piano does. Pianists will find the experience of collaborating more rewarding. This repertoire is no less beautiful or challenging than the repertoire for solo piano. The difference lies in how the role of the collaborative pianist is defined.

Most collaborative pianists are self-employed. That is, they work out of their own homes or studios and have the freedom—but also the responsibility—to take on whatever amount of work they choose. However, because work may be scarce or irregular, some pianists may wish to work full- or part-time for a music school or conservatory.

The most direct way to get this sort of job is to have attended the school where you wish to work. Instrumental and voice teachers who know you and your work may ask you to play for their students' lessons. Playing for lessons is a kind of first step toward what you can achieve as a collaborator or coach. As your skills develop, you may be able to advance from an accompanying role to a teaching and coaching role. An opera department may hire you to help singers learn roles and master diction problems. Some schools have begun to offer classes for piano/vocal or piano/instrumental duos; you may be asked to teach and coach such groups. Pianists are able to major in accompanying at many conservatories today. These new departments give teachers the opportunity to work with piano students alone, but with a focus on the collaborative literature. Music schools also offer opportunities to teach and coach piano chamber music ensembles.

Summer music festivals are often excellent places to gain experience and make contacts as a collaborative pianist. Various festivals provide different kinds of opportunities. Some festivals that also function as schools, such as the Aspen Music Festival, accept pianists as students and then provide them with the opportunity to earn money playing for the lessons of instrumental and vocal students. Other festivals hire pianists outright to play for opera rehearsals and to help singers learn music. The term for such pianists is *repetiteur*. Depending upon whether the pianist is hired to play in a workshop situation or for a professional production, he or she may be required to do more or less coaching—that is, working on language, diction, and style—rather than purely providing an accompaniment. Playing in a summer music festival may also lead to winter employment in a conservatory. Thomas Muraco, a pianist based in New York, relates that his first job there was playing at Juilliard for the late singer and teacher Jennie Tourel, whom he had met and played for at the Aspen Festival.

Coaching and teaching at a school offer the advantages of a steady income and, possibly, medical and other benefits. There is also the chance to make contacts and perhaps to perform. In addition, even a part-time association with a school can give structure to a "free-lance" life-style, particularly during the period in which one is still establishing oneself as a professional pianist.

The difficulty of establishing solid professional credentials as a collaborative pianist cannot be overemphasized. It is a highly competitive field; yet an even greater hindrance may be that this sector of the performing arts is not covered by professional managements. The reason for this is in part economic. Collaborative pianists do not earn large enough fees to warrant the services of a management. At the same time, it is often only by coming to know managers that pianists can get work; managers will recommend pianists to artists of their roster. An informal but very real network of musical "connections" is crucial to the development of a collaborative pianist's career.

Although managers will recommend pianists for jobs, they will not negotiate fees or other aspects of a contract for them. This being the case, a pianist must develop a great deal of business savvy—knowing how to get what you want and deserve without alienating people who may hire you in the future.

A pianist with whom I spoke estimates that the soloists with whom he works may earn fees nine times as large as his. The difference in fees may be even greater if the soloist is in the superstar category. These figures don't necessarily tell the entire story. The way the music business works, a soloist is hired for a certain fee. Working with that lump sum, the soloist then negotiates with a pianist, paying him or her a fee and expenses. The soloist may also pay a commission to management and his or her own expenses, so that what he or she is able to bank may be far less than the actual contracted fee. This system may make it difficult for a pianist to get a good fee, since the more the pianist is paid, the less the soloist receives. The setup may also contribute to the lack of musical equality between pianist and soloist. Rather than both being hired for an engagement, the soloist is hired and in turn hires a pianist.

This system also forces the pianist to be very flexible about fees. He or she must adjust to the soloist's fee for a given engagement. This means that you could make less than $200 or more than $800 for doing the same kind of job. Rehearsal and coaching fees also vary widely. I know of pianists in New York who charge as little as $9 an hour for rehearsing and coaching, and pianists who charge upwards of $30 an hour. You must make a sober evaluation of your worth and what you can reasonably expect your fellow artists to pay.

Collaborative pianists rarely occupy the limelight, but no one should underestimate their role in the music-making process. For some of you, working as a coach/accompanist will be a step in your development as a soloist or, as we shall see later, as a conductor. For others, collaboration will be a way of life. You should maintain a realistic attitude toward some of the problems and frustrations of this profession. Your life may occasionally seem like one big question, "Am I too loud?" I hope that your experience and your appreciation of your own talents will allow you to answer that question with a resounding "No!"

INSTRUMENTALISTS

Instrumentalists who don't join an orchestra or ensemble and who do not have solo careers may be able to earn most or all of their income as free-lance players. Free-lance players are hired for specific concerts or recording engagements. For instance, they may make up the orchestra for a performance of the *Messiah* by a chorus that has no permanent orchestra of its own. Some concert series occasionally program a piece using a chamber orchestra and call on free-lance musicians to make up this orchestra. Churches present Bach cantata concerts, hiring free-lance instrumentalists for the ensemble. Classical musicians, particularly string players, may get work in commercial music as backup for records or commercials. Occasionally more off-beat jobs come along. P.D.Q. Bach hires free-lance players for his yearly concerts. Many players enjoy the chance to do something purely fun like this.

Free-lance instrumentalists are members of the American Federation of Musicians, which sets the standards for rehearsal, salary, and other conditions that may apply to a particular job. The most recent figures for free-lance playing are $12.50 per hour for rehearsals and $60 per performance. Players with large instruments are reimbursed for the expense of transporting their instruments; in some cases transportation is provided.

If you are hired for a job that includes one performance and three hours of rehearsal, you will earn $97.50. Simple arithmetic will tell you that you would need to play several such jobs each week just to survive in a city such as New York or Los Angeles. Again, those are the only two cities in which you could hope to make a living as a free-lance instrumentalist. Any major city has some free-lance opportunities but certainly not enough out of which to carve a livelihood. New York has more live performing opportunities, Los Angeles more film and recording work. Yet even if you do settle in one of those cities, you have no guarantee of getting enough free-lance work to make ends meet.

Contractors do the hiring for free-lance playing jobs. As we saw in the chapter on commercial music, contractors are often players or former players who have entered the profession as a way to earn extra money on a steadier basis. Contractors know about good free-lance players by having worked with them as colleagues. A natural tendency is to call upon the same reliable people again and again. You are lucky if you have played with or for a contractor, or if you went to school with him or her. Or you may have a friend who can introduce you to a contractor or recommend you for a job. If none of these options exists, it may be very difficult to establish yourself as a free-lance player and work steadily.

"Steady work" is also something of an ideal situation. A free-lance violinist who is well established in New York says, "Some weeks I work constantly—concerts, recording sessions—I don't get a break. But then, nothing for weeks." Some players are able to earn enough to tide them over during dry periods; many collect unemployment insurance or look for other work. Recent developments in high technology have created a whole battery of part-time or temporary jobs in fields such as word-processing and computer programming. Any large office will have a number of performing artists working at such jobs. Bartending and waiting on tables are also options, because work shifts tend to be flexible and the pay is good. You may not like to think of a highly trained and qualified musician having to do this kind of work to make ends meet, but it is a fact of life for most of us.

Free-lance players must be technically skilled, musically sensitive, and adaptable to many different types of rehearsal and performing situations. One day you may play baroque trumpet for a Bach cantata. The next day you may form part of the orchestra for a visiting dance troupe, followed by a recording session for a popular vocalist's new album. You must sight-read extremely well and be able to hold your own when a conductor must focus his or her limited energies elsewhere. Some people may find this pace, this moving around from job to job, wearying. Others may find it difficult to have a fulfilling musical experience when you work for such short periods of time with each group. I have heard certain string players refer to their free-lance work as "bowing for dollars!"

On the other hand, free-lance work offers a great deal of variety, the chance to work with some of the best of your colleagues, and a certain amount of flexibility that can be very helpful to you. You may look upon free-lance playing as one step in your development toward a solo career or a position with an orchestra or a chamber group. Free-lance playing can allow you the freedom to practice and commit yourself to future musical goals if that is the path you have chosen. In and of itself, it is a viable alternative for many of you who aspire to performing careers.

SOLOIST

The solo voice of an instrument rising out of the orchestra in a concerto, interweaving with a second voice in a sonata, or singing in isolated splendor in an unaccompanied work can be a thrilling and inspiring sound. Soloists command our undivided attention and our enthusiastic loyalties, and with good reason. They have superb talents, and they pour these into their music-making. They show us that every note, every rest in music has a meaning, and they make that meaning manifest to us. Such people, those who have successful solo careers, are few and far between.

If you are going to have a solo career, the chances are that you are well on your way to achieving it. You will have started playing your instrument at a young age. Encouraged by your teachers and parents, you have invested long hours in practice and study. You have performed in public, and you may have entered local competitions. You may have attended music camps during the summer or have gone to Europe with a youth orchestra. Your choice of college or conservatory will be influenced by the presence of a particular teacher or by the school's proximity to resources and institutions that can further your progress.

The point is that music will already be the ruling force in your life. Music imposes a discipline with which you must be thoroughly familiar and which you must fully accept before you attempt a solo career. Before it is acknowledgment and fame, before it is art and expression, music is work, work, and more work. Of course, we've all read about the prodigies to whom the most difficult technical feats come easily. Yet even they must work for the mental discipline to make a great performance happen. The prodigies, at any rate, are the exceptions to the rule. Even the most talented instrumentalists must practice continually. They "practice so as not to have to practice," as the saying goes. That is, they work at a piece until it becomes part of them, so as to be able to make a performance seem an effortless outpouring of sound and expression.

At this stage of your development, one of the most important things you can do is to find and work with a good teacher. A "good" teacher is good at many levels. First, he or she must be good for *you*; that is, the two of you must be able to have a constructive working relationship. There must be mutual respect for the teacher and pupil roles and a willingness on your part to commit yourself wholeheartedly to what the teacher has to say. Of course, you can do this only if you respect your teacher's way of thinking about and making music. This respect is a hard-to-define combination of your subjective evaluation—your gut feeling—about what a teacher has to say, and objective judgments of a teacher's value based on your own investigation and the opinions of people you trust.

Your teacher must also be someone who understands what it is to have a solo career: the standards of excellence, the performer's commitment, the strains and the rewards of the life-style. Only if your teacher has a sense of these factors will he or she be able to give you a realistic sense of what it takes. Your teacher may have to push you at a frustrating point in your training. You may not be able to see the light at the end of the tunnel, but he or she must see it and must know how to work for it.

A teacher's experience of the music world is also invaluable at the stage in which you plan the shape of your career. Should you accept a certain engagement, enter a competition, make a concert tour of the Far East? Financial, temporal, and artistic elements all come into play here, and it can be a confusing tangle of competing interests to sort out. You need someone who is savvy and yet who has your best interests at heart to help you make crucial decisions along the way.

The issue of how you will organize your career is premature, however, until we have explored how you get to the point where the music world regards you seriously as a soloist. I think we have touched often enough on the matters of talent and hard work. You have to be good enough to compete successfully with those who are having solo careers today. You also have to take your talent and render it into a finished product. Not that you ever *finish* your work, but you must achieve that combination of discipline, experience, and personal style that will enable you to stand up to the rigors of solo performing.

While you are training, you must also begin to develop the network of musical connections that will help you throughout your career. At music camps and summer festivals you will meet established professionals as well as your peers, some of whom will be your fellow performers in the future. Youth orchestras also provide fine performing experiences and can lead to other performing opportunities. The violinist and conductor Alexander Schneider puts together an orchestra of talented student players each year, which presents concerts in the New York area during the Christmas season. A young violinist who worked with Schneider later accepted

Rudolf Serkin's invitation to play with him at the White House. At your college and conservatory your teacher and other professors whom you get to know may be able to recommend you for competitions, fellowships, or jobs.

You may have to pursue other musical opportunities while you work at your solo career. We have already seen that many instrumentalists free-lance to support their continued studies. An aspiring solo violinist in New York recently accepted a position with a well-known string quartet. He has continued to do some solo work and has not ruled out the option of going back to a full-time solo career. His is an unusual case, because, as we have seen, it is very tricky to try to combine a professional chamber music career with anything else. Some performers, such as the pianists Charles Rosen and Samuel Lipman, write books and articles on musical subjects. Many players take private students or look for teaching positions at a music school, conservatory, or college. You may *need* this teaching income for quite a while as you build a solo career. At the point at which you are making enough money playing to support yourself, you may find yourself too deeply involved in teaching to give it up. Further, your growing reputation will make you all the more sought after as a teacher; you will then have to confront the issue of balancing teaching and performing that we discussed earlier.

Competitions are a fact of life for today's aspiring soloists. The number and variety of competitions proliferate with each successive year; now, not only pianists, but violinists, violists, cellists, flutists, guitarists, singers, and others can enter any one of a number of competitions, many of which are held annually. A recent article on competition states that most concert performers under the age of forty, active in the United States today, have won or have placed in major competitions.

It bears repeating that winning a competition does not guarantee your success as a performer, but it does provide an opportunity for you to make yourself known to the public and the music world. Managers may become interested in signing you on. Concert promoters are more likely to hire a competition winner than someone without those credentials. Part of winning a competition may be the opportunity to give a well-publicized recital at a fine concert hall, with a review in a major newspaper guaranteed. Such a review is another important credential for a young performer. Competition prize money can help to ease the burden of career-related expenses. The International American Music Competition, sponsored by the Rockefeller Foundation and Carnegie Hall, offers a $10,000 First Prize. The Peabody–Mason Prize for pianists consists of two full years of support ($1,000 per month for 24 months) and major recitals in New York and Boston. Competitions are held not only in North America, but in South America and Europe as well. You and your teacher must decide which competitions you will enter and how you will prepare for them.

Some performers promote their own concerts. You can hire a concert management service for the one-time job of organizing your recital. This service will take care of all publicity and logistical matters and make sure that the press attends. While it may cost you more than $1,000, it can be a way to gain visibility even if you haven't won a competition.

Fine, you say, but where does one get the money for such an expenditure? Find a patron, someone may answer—and they may be quite serious. Of course, the days are long gone when the Medicis of Florence opened their homes and purses to talented young artists. However, there may be individuals or groups who can and will give you financial support in your career. Men's and women's clubs, religious or ethnic organizations, businesses and corporations may have funds available to help you study or launch your career. You must explore these avenues carefully, not only to find out what options are open to you, but to understand fully the terms and conditions of any such arrangement. As a young artist, you should not hesitate to accept the proper kind of help from the right sources. The arts are not, for the most part, subsidized by the government of this country, and so we need private means of support. Just be sure you know what sort of arrangement you are entering into.

Certain groups and foundations offer such support in a formal way, as yearly grants for which you may apply. In the past, the Martha Baird Rockefeller Foundation and the Fulbright Foundation made money available to young performers. At the present time, the future of both of these funding sources is in doubt. It is to be hoped that other foundations will take their place. Local and state Councils on the Arts, and the National Endowments for the Arts and Humanities may also make some support available to young musicians. Until recently, the Comprehensive Education and Training Act (CETA) provided opportunities for young artists to train and perform. Perhaps this program will be reinstated in the future.

When you have begun to establish yourself as a performer by any or all of the routes mentioned above, you will start looking for management. This means that management must also be looking for you. That is, you cannot simply knock on a manager's door and say, "Listen to me and then sign me on!" A management must have an initial interest in hearing you, either because of a recent award or concert, or because of a well-placed recommendation. Not every performer is signed on by the biggest and best-known managements. A small management may grow into a large firm, and you may be one of the artists who help to build its reputation. What a management needs is clout—the ability to get you good engagements and good fees, as well as to promote you in an aggressive but positive way. Deciding on a management is a crucial step in your career. Think carefully and consult musical colleagues you trust *before* you make a move. Don't act precipitously or out of fear that nothing better will come along. If you're good, something better *will* come along; if you're not, the best management in the world won't be able to help you.

Travel will play a large part in your life as a performer. Musicians visit the small towns and isolated sections of this country and other parts of the world, bringing their art to the millions of aficionados who cannot afford to maintain permanent performing institutions where they live. At the top of the profession, performers spend time in major cities, appearing with their orchestras or giving recitals in their great halls. Whether you play in a church, a high school auditorium, or a concert hall, a concert tour often entails covering great distances in a short period of time and playing night after night in new surroundings. Traveling to perform is a true test of your mettle. You must learn to husband your energy and concentration, to prevent yourself from being distracted by inconveniences and delays, and to adapt yourself to all kinds of performing conditions. Pianists have encountered pianos that have been allowed to fall into utter disrepair. Instrumentalists find that the temperature of a hall fluctuates wildly, wreaking havoc on intonation and even causing cracks in wood instruments. The Heifetz's of the world may cancel under such conditions, but most of us don't have that option. As a world traveler, too, you will come to realize that most of the world lacks the resources of the capital cities of America and Europe. You may have to experience inconvenience and discomfort to a greater or lesser degree in order to bring music to parts of the world where it is a rare gift.

From the foregoing discussion, you may have begun to realize that, even in the narrow and specialized world of concert performance, there are different degrees of making it. There are the legends, such as Horowitz, Heifetz, Oistrakh, and Perlman, who are or have been more or less able to pick and choose where, what, and how they will play. Such performers earn $10,000 and more per performance, sometimes much more. Then there is a level of players who make occasional appearances with major orchestras but also do much of their playing in less well-known arenas. Many younger artists and most major competition winners fall into this category. These people are for the most part well established as performers, and some may achieve superstar status.

Other artists fall into a third category. They do not perform with major orchestras in major halls. Rather, they do virtually all of their performing in small concert series, with local orchestras and community groups. Often this is a stage through which young performers pass on their way to bigger careers. However, some do not move past this stage, and so you will also find older performers at this level. For them, solo performing may provide only a part of their income. They are likely to have active teaching careers and may appear often in chamber music concerts as part of an ensemble. Salaries are difficult to ascertain for solo performers. We hear most about what the superstars ostensibly make, but we probably don't hear the whole story. People at each end of the music business are reluctant to discuss fees because they change all the time and because they differ so greatly from artist to artist.

Not all instruments offer the potential on which to build a solo career. Piano and violin come to mind most readily as solo instruments. The most solo repertoire has been written for them, because they have proven themselves to be such versatile instruments. Among the strings, 'cello ranks next, followed by viola. Some soloists, such as Oscar Shumsky, perform on both violin and viola, but there are few solo violists among today's performers.

The flute is enjoying a wave of popularity as a solo instrument. Jean-Pierre Rampal cultivated this trend and has been followed, perhaps even surpassed, by James Galway. Ransom Wilson, Paula Robinson, and Eugenia Zukerman are some American solo flutists. The flute has a varied repertoire, tending heavily toward baroque and contemporary works. There may be no flute music on the level of a Brahms violin concerto, but the flute is very adaptable. Rampal and Ransom Wilson have both done substantial work transcribing literature of other instruments for the flute. Galway and Rampal have recorded albums of jazz and popular music, and Eugenia Zukerman appears extensively in chamber music concerts.

A handful of guitarists have built fine solo careers for themselves. A very few clarinet, oboe, and horn players perform as soloists. Many of these are Europeans who had already established careers abroad before coming to this country. A trumpet player such as Gerard Schwarz, former principal trumpet of the New York Philharmonic, appears as a soloist in many works requiring baroque trumpet, but one can hardly hope to have a career as a solo trumpeter. Double bass, bassoon, percussion—for all of these instruments a few concerti and other solo pieces exist, but they are rarely performed, and then most often by the principal of that section of an orchestra. As a musician, be realistic about your chances for a solo career. As an instrumentalist, be realistic about the potential of your instrument as a solo instrument.

SINGERS

We have looked at singers in two earlier parts of this book: cantors and other religious music singers, and jingle singers in the commercial music chapter. Singers of classical music are birds of a rather different feather. Their training differs greatly from that of pop singers and, in many cases, of cantors as well. Classically trained singers use their voices in a unique way. Their voices, more accurately their entire bodies, become instruments. Unlike pop singers, for whom the microphone is integral to achieving their particular sound and style, classically trained singers must create all dynamic and expressive nuances with their bodies alone. Unlike cantors, who do one kind of singing, classical singers sing in a variety of styles and genres. This requires formidable technique as well as the strength and coordination of an athlete.

If you have ever sung in a mixed chorus, you know that there are four basic types of singing voice: soprano, alto, tenor, and bass. A further breakdown with which you may be familiar occurs in the lower voices: altos may be divided into mezzo-sopranos and contraltos, and basses into baritones and basses. In fact, there are more vocal gradations than those, based upon the size (also known as the weight) of the voice, its overall quality, its agility, and other criteria. These finer gradations apply most often to opera singers. For instance, no one woman will ever sing Violetta in Verdi's *La Traviata* and Isolde in *Tristan and Isolde* of Wagner. One role calls for what is known as a lyric coloratura soprano and the other for a Wagnerian soprano. One voice is high and fairly light and agile, whereas the other is heavier and more comfortable in a slightly lower range. In like manner, the roles of Papageno and Sarastro, in Mozart's *The Magic Flute*, are both for low male voices. Yet Papageno is written for a high baritone and Sarastro for a true bass. You will learn more about these distinctions as your vocal studies progress and your teacher and you begin to decide what type of voice you have.

Classically trained singers in this country perform many different kinds of music. The economics of the music business dictate, however, that if you want to sing full-time you will be involved with opera. Exceptions to this rule are very rare. Singing in opera could mean singing chorus or as a soloist. Other professional singing opportunities include a small amount of choral work, vocal chamber music (including early music and contemporary music ensembles), recital, and oratorio singing. You may do several of these things in combination or combine singing with teaching or other part-time work. The financial picture is much the same as in other parts of the music business: a few people make it very big, and the rest struggle to make ends meet.

Singing is one of the few performing arts that does not entail training from an early age. In fact, singers are discouraged from beginning their studies until their voices and bodies have matured. This can be as late as eighteen or even later. Now, this does not mean that you can wake up one morning next week and decide to be a singer. Most singers have had a good musical background on instruments—piano is especially helpful as it facilitates your learning music (you can hear the accompaniment as well as your own line). Further, you must have a vocal instrument with natural beauty and potential. Almost anyone will benefit in some way from vocal training, but training cannot give a great voice to a person whose basic vocal equipment is not good. Training can transform a pleasing voice into an instrument of great power and capacity. This transformation is a rigorous process and requires strength as well as discipline. That is why you are encouraged to wait before beginning vocal studies.

To make your voice a singing instrument, you will need to develop several things. You will work to make your voice resonant: to use the bones and cavities of your head as vibrating chambers to create a full and penetrating sound. You will develop breath support and control. Air is the fuel on which the vocal engine runs. Your torso and chest cavity must become a kind of tank, feeding air in a steady stream through your throat, past your vocal cords, into your resonating chambers and out.

Singers also work for consistency of sound. They work to modulate vowels and consonants so as to create a smooth line. Classical singers also work to eliminate the "break" that occurs naturally in all voices. In other styles of singing a break can be used very effectively. You can hear a break in the voice of a singer like Joni Mitchell, or in many musical theater singers, who have a "belt" voice in the lower registers and switch into "head" voice as they move through their break and past it. A great controversy exists in singing circles about the break in the voice—how one should deal with it, what actually causes it. I'm not going to become embroiled in that debate here; there are any number of books on vocal technique that you can read if you are interested. The point is that classical music is written for the voice as if a break did not exist. A classically trained voice should have a consistent sound from its lowest to its highest extremes. Working through a break is an important but often difficult task for singer and teacher.

Teachers and the teaching of singing are another source of controversy among singers. You need to *learn* how to sing classically. That is, you need a teacher, but how do you find a good one? Vocal technique is not something you can see. It all takes place internally, in the vibrating of your vocal cords, the creating of resonance, the shaping of sound. A teacher cannot move your vocal cords the way one can move a pianist's fingers or a violinist's bow arm. Voice teachers rely in great part on images. Of course, there are many things one can physically demonstrate. You can see how your body fills with air and your diaphragm moves to allow that air to flow. You can do exercises to strengthen your jaw and make your tongue flexible. Yet there is also, as any singer will tell you, a "mystique" of vocal technique, hard to define but greatly sought after.

Well, you might say, you may not be able to *see* what good singing looks like, but you *must* be able to hear it. I'll look for a teacher who sings well, or who trains students whose voices are good. I wish I could say it were so straightforward. Yet there is far from general agreement on what good singing is. You can hear so many different kinds of singing today. Some people go so far as to claim that no one sings well today; they claim that the art of singing died in the nineteenth century, when the last bloom of the *bel canto* style faded. Music critics don't agree on what good singing is. Neither do conductors, and voice teachers and singers certainly don't. Some singers make lovely round sounds, but everything sounds the same —vowels, consonants, it's all one beautiful mush. Others have flawless diction, yet their voices lack a certain fullness and richness. Some voices have little projection, or bite, and some have a sharp metallic edge. These are not just the differences that occur from voice to voice, but a reflection of widely divergent philosophies on singing and voice teaching.

So how do you decide what's best for you? This is a very important decision, because you will study voice in some way throughout your life as a singer. You may not have the same teacher throughout your career, but I am also not a believer in constantly switching teachers in vain hope of finding a quick way to fathom the "mystique" of vocal technique. My advice is to use your common sense. Does what a voice teacher says make sense to you? Are you comfortable singing in the way he or she prescribes? Singing requires exertion, but it should not cause strain or tension. Are you developing vocal resonance, breath control, and consistency? Are you able to master songs and arias of increasing technical difficulty? Keep your ears and your mind open.

After this long discussion of singing technique, I have to caution you that vocal technique is only one aspect of good singing. You also need a highly developed sense of musicality, an understanding of style, and a facility with the languages in which you sing.

Beginning with languages, the ideal and rare situation would be to speak and understand the languages, such as German, French, and Italian, that you will use extensively as a classical singer. Barring that, you must be able to pronounce them idiomatically and to understand enough of their construction to be able to make a *word-for-word* translation of what you are singing. If you absolutely can't come up with a translation, find someone who can, because nothing is less convincing than singers who get that glassy-eyed stare of noncomprehension as they warble away words that mean nothing to them. On the other hand, nothing is more exciting than a singer who lets you understand every word, every syllable of what he or she is singing. As far as pronunciation is concerned, you should become familiar with the International Phonetic Alphabet (IPA). IPA is a system of symbols, each of which corresponds to a sound. For example, "a" is the sound of F*a*ther. It is also the sound of p*a*dre. You can apply the symbols to any language, so as to be able to understand the pronunciation in terms of sounds common to all languages.

Style, for singers, is harder to achieve. Much of what we sing in America today derives from a tradition that is essentially nineteenth-century and European. There are German *Lieder,*

French *mélodies,* and Italian opera. European musicians are weaned on this music. They are steeped in it and come by their sense of style quite naturally. The languages of classical singing are their native languages; the music has surrounded them in formal and informal ways all of their lives. These art forms have been transplanted to American soil. They thrive here, but they are not indigenous. American singers must work hard to approximate the natural environment of their European counterparts. They should listen to recordings of all kinds and attend performances by singers who have a great understanding of their genre: Christa Ludwig in *Lieder,* Placido Domingo in Italian opera, Régine Crespin in French vocal music, to name only a few. They should gain background on historical traditions in singing and read biographies of composers and singers. Their training may also include time spent in Europe, but more on that later.

I have had endless arguments with people as to whether or not musicality can be learned. I always agree that you can help people refine the way they shape a phrase. You can point out the subtle effect of accenting certain beats. You can discuss and analyze different ways of attacking a note. Yet there is a fundamental grace and passion of expression in music, a conviction and a statement of your innermost being that are the essence of musicality, and I doubt whether these things can be taught. For singers, musicality as the expression of something within you is all the more important because singing comes so directly from your body, from you. People will recognize and respond to your musicality. You, in turn, must allow it to have its full expression. A solid technique, understanding of languages, and sensitivity to style will allow this to happen.

Once you have brought together the disparate elements of vocal preparation, you can think about singing professionally. You will need to make certain decisions about the kind of career to which you aspire, where and how you'd like to live, and the kind of music you want to sing. For instance, as mentioned before, if you want to sing full-time and you believe you have a chance to be successful, you may wish to pursue an operatic career. If that is the case, you must be prepared to make this career the absolute priority of your life. You may have to travel or live in other parts of the country or perhaps in Europe. You must be able to pursue any opportunity to sing, take endless auditions, and work constantly to improve your technique, understanding of languages, and acting ability and to expand your repertoire of roles. We'll discuss specific steps you will take as you pursue an operatic career later; for now I wanted merely to indicate the commitment you will need to make as differentiated from other kinds of singing. An operatic career takes second place to nothing. You may have to postpone marriage, planning a family, financial security, and other aspects of "settling down" while you establish your career.

An operatic career may not be a realistic choice for you, both because of the commitment involved, and because it is such a competitive field. One alternative that exists within the opera world is to sing as a member of an opera chorus. In the larger American companies this can mean full-time employment, at least during the season. Opera companies hold occasional auditions, but chorus members tend to hold their jobs for many years. This means that the field is a competitive one, particularly in the larger companies where the terms of employment are most favorable. Many companies do call on the services of extra chorus members for certain productions. You may be able to get work this way, but it would have to be in addition to other singing work. Some chorus members work their way up through the ranks to sing small roles. Others perform in other capacities when they are not singing at the opera. Opera choruses are rarely over-rehearsed, and, particularly if the production is an old and familiar one, chorus members may have few responsibilities other than appearing at the stage door early enough to put on makeup and costume before the performance. If you sing in an opera chorus, you may go on tour with your company, but you will not have to travel to singing engagements throughout the season as a soloist does.

There is little opportunity for other kinds of professional chorus work in this country. (An exception may be religious choirs in certain parts of the country.) Twenty and more years ago, there was a more popular and viable tradition of choral singing, which meant work not only for choristers but for soloists as well. Today most choral performances are presented by fine amateur choirs, college choirs, and some groups such as the Chicago Symphony Chorus, which combine some professional with amateur singers. The Gregg Smith Singers are a small professional chorus of sixteen to twenty voices, based in New York, but they represent about the extent of professional choral opportunities in the United States.

There are some professional ensembles that specialize in a certain type of music—Renaissance or contemporary, for instance. These groups often use singers, alone or in small groups. Some singers build their careers on the performance of this type of music, and it influences the way they train and use the voice. Early music, for instance, requires a small, pure sound with very little vibrato. An early music singer will probably become something of an expert in ornamentation, particularly for baroque music. Much contemporary music requires a great deal of range and flexibility of the voice. You may have to make nonsinging sounds or sing a very low note followed immediately by an extremely high note. Some contemporary pieces employ a technique known as *Sprechstimme,* which is a kind of pitched declamation midway between singing and speech. Singers who develop these specialties will probably find that they have a lot of work; however, they may not be high-paying jobs. This repertoire has a loyal but limited following and is better performed in small halls. Another drawback is that, once you have established a reputation as an early music or contemporary specialist, you may have trouble finding singing work in other areas. People tend to typecast you, and that is a difficult image from which to break free.

Oratorio and recital singing are two other career possibilities for singers. Unfortunately, both have declined in popularity in recent times. Some optimistic lovers of this music predict a comeback, but the fact is that there is less demand for oratorio and recital in the United States than there was twenty years ago. We have already noted this trend in the decline of professional choruses. Singers were once able to base much of their career on appearances as oratorio soloists. Popular vocal "quartets" would be engaged together for numerous performances of the Beethoven Ninth Symphony, the *Missa Solemnis,* the Verdi *Requiem*, the Bach B Minor Mass, and so on. Today some singers still appear regularly in oratorio, often in churches or with amateur choruses. Such singers probably also hold positions as voice teachers at a college or conservatory, or teach privately. When a large orchestra mounts a choral work, they tend to hire operatic superstars as the soloists. These singers may not be the best suited to the style, but they draw at the box office.

The oratorio singers of the last generation were often popular recitalists as well. Indeed, in years past there was more of a tradition of versatility among singers than there is today. Of course, today's opera stars always present the requisite recital or two each season, yet they are often not at home in such a forum. Twenty-five years ago, many singers moved from opera to oratorio to recitals and contemporary and baroque music with ease and expertise. There was a thriving tradition of recital singing, and fine recitals were in great demand. Now, for reasons of taste and perhaps economics, the intimate and often cerebral evening a recital offers is less in demand than the gala "concert of the century" featuring all of your favorite opera stars, violin virtuosi, and famous conductors in one fabulous evening. I recently attended master classes given by Gérard Souzay, the famed French baritone and recitalist. At one particularly poignant moment, he turned to his listeners and asked "When will the age of recitals return to America?" It was a question for which no one had an answer.

Professional vocal recitals are presented under several kinds of situations today. Many singers rent a hall in a major city and present themselves in debut recitals, hoping to receive a favorable review that will add to their credentials and make them a known quantity to managements. Competition prizes often include a sponsored recital with good publicity, in a fine hall. These are a few recital series around the country, often at museums and on university campuses. There are the superstar recitals mentioned earlier. There are also some unique programs such as Community Concerts and Affiliate Artists, in which singers and other musicians are hired to travel and perform (in some cases to live) in parts of the country not normally exposed to classical music. These are prestigious and competitive programs, which provide an invaluable experience for a few American musicians.

Singers work to establish themselves in many of the same ways as do other professional musicians. They audition, enter competitions, and, if they are pursuing solo careers, try to find management. Singers can gain good experience and exposure by singing with the many small semiprofessional and professional opera companies that thrive in cities today. Some of these companies cannot afford to pay their singers, but others do offer small fees. Some tour around their area, and many performances are attended by managers and receive major reviews.

Many singers also earn money and expand their skills by singing in churches and synagogues. Much of this is choral work, but in some instances you may be a church soloist. If that is the case, you will solo with your church choir when it presents special oratorio concerts, as well as for the regular Sunday services. In big cities, these jobs are very hard to come by, because people tend to hold onto them for years. You can audition for a church or synagogue job, in some cases, by applying directly to the music director. In many cases, however, you must go through a church agent, a person who functions much like a contractor. A teacher or your singer colleagues should be able to tell you whom you should contact in your area.

Many American opera singers are advised to go to Europe to establish careers. Small professional opera houses flourish in most European cities. They present operas in repertory and are well and enthusiastically attended throughout their seasons. In Europe, many opera singers perform only with their home company. Although they don't achieve the stardom of singers with international careers, many more work steadily as opera singers than is the case in the United States. The very fact that the Europeans are open to having American singers work in their houses indicates that more opportunity exists in Europe. Some American singers establish themselves in Europe but hope to return and make names for themselves in the United States. Some spend their entire professional lives in Europe, finding the American music world too difficult to break into. Many black opera singers have felt that they have encountered less prejudice from European opera companies and so have chosen to sing there rather than fight what they consider to be a discriminatory system.

Singing in Europe has, of course, its advantages and its drawbacks. On the plus side, it means steady work and the opportunity to live in Europe, perfect your foreign languages, become familiar with a different culture. At the same time, you will probably be far away from friends and family, often for years at a time. An artistic drawback to the European system has to do with its repertory policy and the way singers are classified. In Europe, all singers are assigned to a *Fach*, or vocal category. That category consists of the type of voice you have and the operatic roles that type of voice can sing. The Europeans define these categories rather narrowly, and they absolutely disallow crossing over from one *Fach* to another. This means that you may sing the same role over and over again, season in and season out. Even if you think your voice is developing and you have the capacity to attempt a new kind of role, the *Fach* system prevents you from doing so. In the end, some singers are forced to leave Europe to escape from their *Fach* categorization and explore new roles.

Voice teaching is something that almost every singer will undertake at some point during his or her career. Many aspiring singers help to support themselves in this way. Teaching can be fairly lucrative and is flexible from a scheduling point of view. Sometimes it seems as if there are as many teachers as there are singers. Anyone can hang out his or her shingle that says "Voice Teacher" and take on students. There are teachers of all kinds. Some have studied a particular technique such as the Linklater or Lessac methods. Some have great followings due not so much to their teaching ability as to the success of their performing careers. Some, quite frankly, are unqualified to teach and harm their students more than they help them. Voice teachers can charge anywhere from $10 to $100 per lesson. Of course, no one but the most sought-after teachers command the higher fees, but a young singer/teacher could easily earn $20 an hour teaching.

I believe that it is up to each person to hit upon the right balance between his or her own needs and what he or she has to offer as a teacher. Many people want to study singing; not only singers, but actors, dancers, and people in unrelated professions who simply love music. In other words, if you advertise yourself well, you will probably have very little trouble finding students. Because there are so many opinions on what constitutes vocal technique, there are many opinions on what makes a good teacher. You must, in great part, be your own judge in this matter. Are you helping your students to understand more about their voices and vocal technique? Are you helping them to recognize what good singing is as well as helping them to sing better? Keep such questions in mind if you are considering teaching voice.

One way that you can develop your own teaching skills is to observe the work of your own teacher. We have discussed the importance of a teacher in the section on solo performing. For singers, a coach can be almost as important a person as a teacher. A coach, as we saw in the section on collaborative pianists, may help singers to learn music, to improve their diction and understanding of texts, and to develop an interpretation and a stylistically authentic way of performing a piece. A coach may accompany you in auditions and collaborate with you on recitals, so that your relationship with him or her has many levels. A coach and singer may, at different times, be teacher and student, colleagues, friends, and even employee and employer. You may work with only one or a very few coaches in your entire professional life. The bonds of trust and respect and the ability to make music together must be very strong.

Choosing singing as a career means that you may make many other choices regarding your life. Physical health and strength will be of great importance to you—your instrument maintenance, as it were. Singers should never smoke and must in general be moderate eaters and drinkers as well. The myth of the fat opera singer is most definitely a myth. Exercise, plenty of sleep, appropriate dress for the weather, these are all things that should be part of a singer's routine. Your singing will also influence many of your personal relationships. You will very likely have close and long-standing relationships with a teacher and a coach. You may also work frequently with a particular conductor. You will need a supportive spouse and family, particularly if your career requires you to be away from home for long periods of time. A singer's art is inseparable from a singer's discipline, and this applies to you whether you are an opera star, a voice teacher, or a chorister. The extent of discipline required will weed out all but the most dedicated aspirants. If you can stick with it, there may well be a place for you as a professional singer.

COMPOSERS

In today's music world, the terms "popular" and "contemporary" connote two very different types of music, different audiences, different kinds of composers. There are songwriters, composers of popular music, such as Stephen Sondheim or the late John Lennon. Then there are composers of contemporary music such as John Cage or Elliott Carter. If you know any of the work of these four men, you can understand the distinction between "popular" and "contemporary." Occasionally the two realms meet. A piece such as George Gershwin's *Rhapsody in Blue* comes to mind immediately. The composer Edgard Varèse has recently become known to rock 'n' roll fans because of Frank Zappa's interest in him. Laurie Anderson is a composer who has achieved international recognition as a multimedia performance artist; she has a large following among devotees of New Wave art and music. Leonard Bernstein also has had success in both fields, as the composer of works such as *West Side Story,* and the *Chichester Psalms.*

For the most part, however, "contemporary" music has an intention and appeal quite opposite to that of "popular" music. Music written today for orchestras, chamber ensembles, choruses—that is, music that falls into the tradition of "classical" music—more often than not has little popular appeal. Few pieces, even those that are premiered by major orchestras or other groups, work their way into the standard repertoire. Fewer still are successful from a financial point of view. These are all things to consider if you are contemplating a career as a composer.

If this sounds grim, think for a moment about the life of Mozart. Mozart lived a hand-to-mouth existence and died practically a pauper. He had to fight to get performances of many of his finest works, some of which were almost forgotten after their premieres. If he had given up for failing to win the eighteenth-century equivalent of a gold record, think of the masterworks we would never have heard.

My point is not that every composer should expect to be destitute, nor that every destitute composer will be a reincarnation of Mozart. Rather, while I can't overemphasize the potential problems and difficulties of being a composer today, I don't want to underemphasize the potential rewards and the need to maintain a viable tradition of composition in America.

I believe it is important for composers to be able to write new works and for those works to be performed. Composers today are wrestling with what Donal Henahan, music critic of the New York *Times*, recently referred to as a crisis of confidence over the very nature of music itself: what it should sound like, what it should express, how it should affect its audience. These are problems that even Mozart didn't face, because they are twentieth-century problems. Donal Henahan writes, "A chart of the grand design of twentieth-century music...would show a narrowing of ambition and a loss of confidence, roughly paralleling the history of wars, depressions and threats of nuclear destruction."

What Henahan is saying is that modern life presents us with certain issues and dilemmas that have no parallel in our experience—such as the threat of nuclear war. Artists have responded to this by questioning the validity of traditional art forms in the face of a changed and changing world. In music, this has meant a questioning of tonality—the system of composition based on seven-note scales in which dissonance is resolved in the recognizable framework of a tonic key and its related keys.

Much contemporary music explores the possibilities of dissonance that does not resolve, of compositions based not on keys but other modes of organization. You may have read about or studied the twelve-tone system in a music history or theory class. It is a way of organizing pitches using the twelve half-steps that are found in any scale. In the twelve-tone system, developed by Arnold Schoenberg, a composer composes a *row*, consisting of all twelve of those pitches arranged in an order he or she chooses. Throughout the composition, this original order or relationship of pitches is preserved, although the pitches may be combined as chords, used in fragments, the row inverted, and so on.

The music that results from this technique of composing sounds quite different from tonal music. It is *atonal*. Although Schoenberg began composing atonal music in the early twentieth century, many people still find it very unfamiliar and difficult to accept in the same context as a Mozart symphony or a Brahms string quartet. While audiences still struggle with the whole concept of atonality, composers have gone off in numerous directions from Schoenberg's work. Electronic music, new instruments, and the inspiration of non-Western music are only a few of the influences that have been brought to bear on contemporary music.

Much contemporary music may seem bewildering, and perhaps much of it is not very good. But I think you have to try to place it in perspective. From all that is being composed today, time will point out works of quality and universality. These will be the guideposts toward a twentieth-century musical style.

Here Mozart comes to mind again. Thousands of operas were composed during his lifetime, many of them more popular in their day than his works. Yet now, when we think of eighteenth-century operas, we think of Mozart's works; the operas of his peers are little more than historical footnotes. Those operas may have been inferior, but they provided the context without which an opera such as *The Marriage of Figaro* would never have been written. Boris Goldovsky, the well-known opera director, tells the story that Mozart went to the premiere of an opera of one of his most popular colleagues. It was apparently a very good work, and well received. Mozart left the performance early, feeling ''ill.'' He began work on *Figaro* the next day, and some of the ideas for its structure can be traced back to the other work, which seemed to inspire both Mozart's envy and his creativity.

Composers today also need a context as they continue exploring basic questions about the nature of music. While they continue to question the validity of tonality, there is no agreement on what constitutes a viable alternative. I believe, however, that only if composers do have a free rein to explore and the opportunity to hear their music and that of their colleagues, can they hope to find those alternatives and make them viable.

Audiences, too, must become more familiar with the atonal language of contemporary music. They must hear enough to be able to accept the beauty of dissonance on its own terms and to be able to distinguish good compositions from mediocre ones. The good compositions should be accepted as part of the standard repertoire, rather than as oddities that receive an obligatory handful of performances, only to be shelved.

Composers today fight an uphill battle on many levels. Like their historical counterparts, they have financial worries and they may have trouble getting their works performed. On top of that, there is the fundamental lack of agreement on musical language. Composers disagree with one another as to what is valid music to be writing today. The audience, on its part, feels alienated by much of what it hears because it is so unfamiliar. The answer to that, however, is to learn the language. Composer and audience must learn to communicate in the language of contemporary music. For composers this means the freedom to work out ideas and to exchange ideas with their colleagues. For the audience, it means developing the capacity to appreciate contemporary music as music and to begin to set standards of quality as we do for other kinds of music.

I've spent a long time on this discussion of contemporary music because I believe that anyone who wants to be a composer today has to understand and accept two very important things. First, a composer must be willing and able to participate in the ongoing debate over what constitutes a valid style (or styles) of twentieth-century music. More important, a composer must firmly believe that he or she has something significant to add to the debate, something essential to say through his or her music. Second, contemporary composers must accept the conclusions arrived at by Schoenberg and others at the beginning of this century: tonal music as it was composed through the end of the nineteenth century cannot be composed today.

I don't mean, of course, that contemporary music must be absolutely atonal. In fact, one of the best trends (in my mind) among some composers today is a reintroduction of elements of tonality into their work. For learning purposes, as well, I think it's invaluable to be able to compose a fugue or a movement in sonata form in a historical style. These are the things that hone a composer's craft, just as a painter studies drawing, or a dancer works for hours at the barre.

The point is that tonal music, which came into its own during the age of Bach, reached its logical conclusions in the music of the late nineteenth century—Mahler, Strauss, Puccini. To compose music such as that today would be to echo a historical form of music, rather than to create music that grows out of the spirit of its time. If you are interested in writing tonal music, you may want to explore the options of songwriting, musical theater, film scores, and so on. In these areas of popular music, tonal composition is alive and well. Here the traditions are different, the music often deriving from folk music or ballads. Jazz also exerts a strong influence on popular music. If you want to write symphonies, concerti, operas, or chamber pieces, these influences may come into play, yet I think that you must accept the dominance of the atonal language of contemporary music.

As a composer, your life will almost certainly focus around a college or conservatory. Your training may take eight years or longer if you opt for a doctoral degree. Many composers choose to do this, so as to be able to continue to work with their teachers. Student composers may also have an easier time putting together a performance of their work at a school than anywhere else. A school can also offer part-time employment to composers, as teachers of ear-training, theory, or music history.

Your own studies will include history, theory, and analysis of music, especially in the first years. At this point, your training is not dissimilar to that of any music major. You will probably attend a seminar in composition in which the faculty, themselves working composers, will discuss aspects of composition each week. You may also participate in a pro-seminar, during which you will present your own compositions for discussion and critique.

As you advance in your studies, your training will take on a different form. You may complete all or most of your classwork. Although you may still attend seminars in composition or composers' forums, much of your work will be done on your own and in private meetings with your composition teacher. The relationship between teacher and student can be extraordinarily intense, involving, as it does, an intimate critique of the student's creative output. The teacher may impose the rigors of rational analysis on something the student sees as in great part the product of inspiration. Egos, as well as ideas, may clash as teacher-composer and student-composer work to turn musical ideas into finished works.

While you are still in school, you can do several things to make yourself known as a composer. You should try to organize performances of your work. You can do this in school concerts, or you can try to interest contemporary music ensembles in your work. If your classmates agree to perform a piece of yours, you will almost certainly become involved in copying scores and parts and organizing and perhaps even directing rehearsals. Getting a professional ensemble can also be a lengthy process. In either instance, you must be prepared to spend a good deal of time and effort in order to get your work played.

Young composers can also apply or be recommended for numerous awards and grants. ASCAP sponsors an annual competition for contemporary pieces. Several composers win each year, and you can submit work more than once, even if you have already won. Music schools themselves offer prizes in composition. Composers may apply to spend time at an artists' colony, such as the MacDowell Colony, where they can work undisturbed on a particular project. All of this sort of aid is awarded on a very competitive basis. You should consult with teachers and others you respect to find out if you are eligible for any of these awards.

This kind of aid can be extremely important, as so much of a composer's time may have to be spent earning an income that will allow him or her to compose. You will not as a rule make money from your compositions per se. You may receive a commission from an individual, a foundation, or a performing group. The Metropolitan Opera, for instance, has commissioned Jacob Druckman to write an opera for an upcoming celebration. Druckman is a well-known contemporary composer and teacher of composition. It is reported that he will receive $150,000 for the work. That is a substantial amount of money, but you must consider that Druckman will spend several years writing the opera. The commission will allow him to support himself while he works.

Your work may be recorded and published. Some composers invest their own money in recordings and publications, not because they hope to see a financial return on their investment, but in order to make their work better known. Others are invited to record and publish, but again, these will hardly be works to appeal to a mass audience as a popular song does. That is not to say that no contemporary pieces gain popular reputations; most of us are familiar with some of the works of Copland, Britten, Menotti, and Barber. Yet the fact is that most contemporary works do have a limited following, which may be made up mostly of other composers and academics.

This being the case, it is more than likely that you will spend much of your time teaching composition at a college or conservatory. Some composers choose a different route. They may teach general music courses at a high school or college. Some call upon their performing talents; I recently met a composer who was playing nightly at a New York City piano bar. What you choose to do will depend upon your own personality and needs. If you see composition as very much an academic discipline, college-level teaching may be where you will find your niche. If you hope to write music with a broader appeal, you may want to work at something removed from "the ivory tower."

It may seem strange to you to think of music as ensconced in an ivory tower. Music plays such an important role in so many of our lives, precisely because it is so accessible on so many levels. Why do many of today's composers write works that are anything but accessible? To get back to my initial point, this apparent quandary has to do with the strange position in which today's composers find themselves. They lack an agreed-upon language in which to express themselves. Each new work represents an experiment, an attempt to find a language that is appropriate to a modern age and yet embodies the universal and affective qualities that make music the art that it is. You must be brave to choose to be a composer today. Not only must you be willing to undertake the search for a musical language, but you must be able to stand firm behind your musical convictions even if some of your colleagues tell you that your musical language sounds like nonsense syllables. Don't expect to grow rich from your labors; you will earn an academic's salary and not much more. But be assured that you will be in the vanguard of the attempt to discover and shape the course of our society's music.

CONDUCTING

Conducting in America is a part of the music world that remains largely dominated by men and, to a somewhat lesser extent, by Europeans. Zubin Mehta, Georg Solti, Carlo Maria Giulini, Sergiu Commissiona, Edo de Waart, Msistislav Rostropovich were all born and trained abroad. In the present generation Americans are vying for at least equal representation as conductors of our great orchestras and opera companies: James Levine, Michael Tilson Thomas, Leonard Slatkin, James Conlon, and Lawrence Foster, to name only a few. Yet women are still struggling to receive serious consideration as conductors. Antonia Brico pioneered as a woman conductor earlier in this century. Her story is the subject of a moving documentary made by Judy Collins, her former pupil. Sarah Caldwell, Eve Queler, and Judith Somogi are among the few women who have had success as opera conductors in this country. Aspiring conductors must be realistic about their chances in a world that retains some of its old notions about who may or may not conduct.

Conducting is a highly competitive profession. As you know, not all musical enterprises require the services of a conductor. Chamber music ensembles and recitals "conduct" themselves. Conductors lead bands, orchestras (of all kinds), and dramatic works of ballet, musical theater, and opera. A single conductor heads up an ensemble that may number 100 people and more. Our finest conductors are in demand not only for their own posts, but as guest conductors the world over. The corps of professional conductors is an elite group indeed.

Most conductors begin their careers as instrumentalists, and many are pianists. Some, like James Levine and Daniel Barenboim, are piano virtuosi and continue to appear in public as piano soloists. The piano is a useful instrument for an aspiring conductor, for several reasons. Many young conductors work as coaches to support themselves and, particularly if they are interested in opera, to learn more about singing and conducting. Some are able to get jobs as assistant conductors with opera companies. These are essentially coaching positions, preparing singers for their work with the actual conductors of the operas they sing. Symphony orchestras also hire assistant conductors, who may work with sections of the orchestra or do preliminary rehearsing. Being a pianist also enables a conductor to read through a score and to work out ideas with at least an approximation of the sound of a work.

Music schools offer programs in conducting at undergraduate and graduate levels. However, the most significant part of your education will undoubtedly be close individual work with a specific conductor or conductors. Many summer music festivals offer conducting fellowships. A small number of student conductors are able to work with renowned conductors in the relatively relaxed atmosphere of a summer festival. Being an assistant conductor may also bring you into close contact with someone well established in the field. In addition, some conductors take on personal assistants, paid or unpaid, who gain firsthand knowledge of the art of conducting at the hands of a master.

Conductors work through managers and agents as do soloists in other performing careers. Conducting engagements may be made years in advance, and the logistical and other aspects of making these arrangements require professional management. The process of getting a management we have observed in other spheres. Managers must hear you, see your résumé and credentials, and be reminded of your presence on the music scene and your readiness, willingness, and ability to take on any engagement. Management will make or break your career, making you a credible presence on the conducting circuit, or no presence at all.

Even before you reach the level where you can consider studying with a Seiji Ozawa or a Leonard Bernstein, you can begin to work with conductors and perhaps to lead groups yourself. A college choir or orchestra may have openings for assistant conductors. You may be able to start a chamber orchestra or vocal ensemble of your own. If there are fine conductors in your area, contact them. Take a few lessons from them and observe them. Attend as many concerts as you can and listen to recordings of great conductors of the past

Zubin Mehta.   *Courtesy the New York Philharmonic*

and present. Read articles on and interviews with famous conductors. Make yourself an expert on the profession.

A conductor needs many qualities, but among the most important are a high level of musical sophistication and an excellent technique. The two go hand in hand, because a good conducting technique permits a conductor to communicate his or her ideas to the
ensemble, and a sophisticated and coherent musical concept will
help to clarify the conductor's indications. In what ways does a conductor lead an ensemble? On the most basic level he or she indicates

the tempo and rhythm of the piece and the dynamics at any given point. A conductor must make sure that the players are following the composer's indications; *i.e.*, to play staccato, legato, accented, and so on. In addition, he or she must clarify any confusing aspects of the score and refine the ensemble's understanding of the markings. For instance, if a composer writes in a ritard or *rubato,* how much should the tempo be stretched? where in the music does this begin and end? There are many kinds of staccato notes. What sort are called for in any given situation? The ensemble looks to the conductor in such cases, and the conductor must have convincing answers.

A conductor must shape each phrase. Does the phrase move forward, or describe an arc, coming to a climax and then tapering off? More than each phrase, a conductor must shape an entire piece. How does each movement relate to the other—what does the *Andante* of the first movement mean in relation to the *Allegro con fuoco* of the final movement? Is the *piano* dynamic indication in a slow movement the same as that in a *Scherzo*?

Perhaps more important, a conductor must provide an underlying meaning—philosophy, if you will—of a piece of music. Many of you have heard of the distinction between programmatic and absolute music. Programmatic music tells a specific story. Operas, of course, are programmatic, as is the music written for ballet. Works such as Beethoven's *Pastoral* Symphony and Berlioz' *Symphonie Fantastique* are programmatic. Absolute music has no specific context, tells no specific story. It offers itself purely as music, allowing the audience to create its own context, draw its own associations, make its own meaning of the sounds it hears. A conductor is the *initial* audience of the piece of music. He or she must create the context, note by note, and as a whole. A conductor must make a piece of absolute music something an audience can understand, without dictating to it an iron-clad and rigid interpretation. If the piece is programmatic, the conductor must have very specific images in mind. Where is the scene the music describes? When does the story take place? Who are the characters? What do they look and sound like? To arrive at these images, a conductor may have to be more than musically astute. History, literature, poetry, and philosophy will play a part in forming a concept of a piece. Ideally, a conductor is something of a Renaissance man. A curious and wide-ranging intellect informs his or her musicianship.

If you don't conduct at the Metropolitan Opera or the Chicago Symphony, where *do* you conduct? We have seen that many music educators are conductors. Whereas some simply take on conducting as another of their many duties, many are talented and inspiring leaders. A high school conductor or even an elementary school conductor may be responsible for a student's decision to go into professional music. Many colleges and conservatories have orchestras of extremely high caliber, led by conductors of equal ability. Conservatory conductors may be conductors who have had extensive professional experience or who are advancing in professional circles. University conductors may be young conductors who accept the position as a stepping-stone to other posts or those who have made a career of working with students.

Summer festivals may also provide opportunities for conductors to gain professional experience. Leonard Bernstein studied and conducted with Serge Koussevitzky at the Tanglewood Festival. Many aspiring opera conductors make their mark at the Santa Fe Opera, held each summer in Santa Fe, New Mexico. Beverly Sills, in her capacity as Artistic Director of the New York City Opera, has committed the company to providing opportunities for young American conductors during the winter season as well.

Community orchestras, small opera companies, and amateur choirs are all groups that employ conductors. Whether you hope to build a bigger career from such work or whether you find your niche at that level, these jobs will not provide you with a full-time income. What else you do to earn money is really up to you. I know conductors who coach and accompany, conductors who also are church choir directors and teachers, conductors who work in music stores, and conductors who are bartenders. I also know conductors who are supported by spouses or receive financial help from their families. Any way you look at it, there are choices and compromises to be made from a financial point of view.

Addressing the money question in the context of conducting careers is quite appropriate, because in a sense there is no limit to the amount of money you could spend getting a conducting career off the ground. There is really no age at which you are too old to make a success as a conductor. In fact, age may often be an asset for a conductor, perhaps adding to the image of a figure of authority, whereas youth has come to dominate so many other parts of the music world. An aspiring conductor may spend years studying, attending summer festivals, applying for grants and fellowships, making tapes of his or her work, traveling to auditions, and so on. All of this takes money, and the whole thing may boil down to, do you have that money, or do you not? Many people may have the talent to conduct. How many have the resources to develop that talent and to support themselves until that talent is recognized? This is a harsh reality of musical life in America. Some of us may have to discontinue our studies, and some may forgo attempting a musical career altogether, for largely economic reasons.

I also continue to believe that talent will rise to the top. That is a belief that must keep many musicians going. Couple that belief with a clear and realistic assessment of the obstacles you must clear. Conducting is a highly visible and glamorous profession. It allows you to use all of your talents—musical, intellectual, and personal—in a most fulfilling way. It is a career in which only a few will succeed at any level. Know what to expect, how far you will need to extend yourself before you can expect any kind of return. That sounds like investment advice, and in a way it is. And, as with any investment, you must be prepared to take certain risks—backed by knowledge and common sense. You must know your own worth and the value of those things to which you aspire.

Chapter VII

Conclusion

Part of writing an educational text is the education, or perhaps the reeducation, of the author. Even if you are a so-called expert on a subject, the process of pulling together your ideas and organizing them into readable form invariably clarifies certain issues and calls others into question.

For me, the issues that emerged over and over again were these: the competitiveness of the music business, the money factor—how much you need and how much you will earn, and the qualities and skills you need to have a career in music.

Music is a competitive business. The competition comes in different degrees, but it exists at every level. A music educator has to compete to get into a Masters program, and then for jobs that diminish in numbers as school systems are forced to cut back arts programs. A free-lance clarinetist competes to get a job in the orchestra playing for the Stuttgart Ballet's tour of the East Coast. A violinist enters a competition, the winning of which could mean being signed on by a prestigious management. A jingle singer auditions for a commercial that could bring in thousands of dollars in residual payments.

It is difficult for people outside of the music business to comprehend the competitiveness that is a day-to-day reality for those in music. For most people, competition is a means to an end. You compete successfully to establish a secure position for yourself in whatever endeavor you have chosen. For music educators, music therapists, and, to some extent, music administrators, competition plays this limited role in their lives. For most performers, however, competition is only as far away as their next engagement. No one really transcends competition in the music world. Even the greatest performers become expendable if their music-making begins to falter. Not only must you accept competition as part of your routine, but you must accept that it may not be fair competition as you understand it in other parts of your life. If you write a good paper, you get an "A." If you work very hard at your job, you get a bonus. Yet you may play or sing spectacularly and fail to get a certain job. Why? Because your look is not right for a certain role, or because they'd rather use someone who has played the part before. A funny combination of objective and subjective criteria influences decisions at all levels of music-making. You accept this and keep plugging away, or you look for another career.

Money and the lack thereof are factors that affect careers in music in many ways. You need money to study and train, and for many that training goes on for years. You need money to support yourself at the stage when you are between being a student and a professional. Again, that stage may last for an extended period of time. You must be prepared to earn only a moderate income or perhaps not even your entire income in almost every musical career, from teaching to performing. You must expect to have high expenses, particularly as a performer, for such things as management, instrument maintenance, and travel. You may need to seek out investors to back a recording or the publication of music. You may apply to foundations for grants to support a research project or to enable you to travel to a competition. You may have to spend time and money training yourself in nonmusical skills so as to support your musical career.

On an organizational level, money becomes an issue because so much of it circulates in the process of any musical undertaking. Nonprofit organizations such as symphony orchestras and opera companies need to find ways to raise great sums to cover their expenses each year. As public sources dry up, private funds must be tapped by sophisticated and wide-ranging fund-raising and development staffs. For money-making businesses, such as managements and record companies, artistic output and profit are intimately related. As a performer, you must realize that you are not only making music, but you are making money for your manager and your producer. Creativity and profitability must operate together, or everyone loses out in the long run.

Of the qualities and skills you need for a career in music, your musical talents are absolutely the bottom line. You must be accomplished, not only in a general way, but in the very specific context of current standards of taste and excellence. No book can help you to acquire talent. You must *believe* in your talent for your own sake and *know* that you are talented from the point of view of those who will judge you.

Talent, however, does not begin to tell the story of what is needed for a musical career. You need to love music and to believe that communication through music is the highest form of communication you will achieve. You must be committed to the notion of your ongoing self-education as a musician. A teacher must constantly refresh ways of imparting basic musical knowledge. A music therapist must develop new techniques to aid mentally and physically disabled patients. A songwriter must come up with fresh tunes and original harmonies; a singer, with a new way to interpret a song. No one ever finishes learning to be a musician. Conductors learn new scores and deepen their understanding of old ones. Jazz musicians work to refine their art of improvisation. A singer strives to give every note, every syllable, every rest, and every nuance its own meaning. No one tells you to do these things. You do them if you are a successful musician, and doing them, in turn, will help you to succeed in a musical career.

Musicians must be tenacious. From some points of view this tenacity may be viewed as obnoxious, but I prefer to cast it in a more positive light. Tenacity means studying diligently and striving for excellence. It means allowing the time for your musical skills to develop and ripen into a mature creative expression. It also means sending out résumés, making phone calls, knocking on doors, and introducing and reintroducing yourself to the right people. Tenacity means always being prepared to accept opportunities, and yet remaining undaunted if those opportunities are few and far between. Tenacity means accepting the foibles of the music world because its joys are so great. It means planting your musical seeds and nurturing them until their network of roots helps to bring your career to fruition.

In this book we have explored some nonperforming careers that were perhaps less familiar to you, as well as many creative and performing careers. Let these discussions serve as a framework for your further exploration of the world of music and musical careers. The music world is always changing, and with it, professional opportunities change. It is also a world open to professional creativity and resourcefulness. If you can see a need for a particular skill or service in the music world, you may be able to create a job for yourself by being able to provide that skill or service. The list of organizations that follows may help you to find out more about areas in which you are interested, or to become acquainted with a new aspect of the infinitely diverse world of music.

Organizations and Institutions to Contact

UNIONS

The American Federation of Musicians is the largest union for musicians in the United States. In addition, you may belong to other unions, depending upon your area of specialization.

American Federation of Musicians
1500 Broadway
New York, NY 10036

American Guild of Musical Artists
1841 Broadway
New York, NY 10036

American Guild of Variety Artists
1540 Broadway
New York, NY 10036

PROFESSIONAL AND TRADE ASSOCIATIONS

American Society of Composers, Authors and Publishers
   (ASCAP)
1 Lincoln Plaza
New York, NY 10024

Broadcast Music, Inc.
320 West 57th Street
New York, NY 10019

Chamber Music America
1472 Broadway, Fourteenth Foor
New York, NY 10018

Dramatists Guild
234 West 44th Street
New York, NY 10018

American Symphony Orchestra League (Orchestra Management
   Fellowship Program)
Post Office Box 669
Vienna, VA 22180

American Musicological Society
201 South 34th Street
Philadelphia, PA 19104

COMMERCIAL MUSIC TRAINING

The New York School for Commercial Music
196 Bleecker Street
New York, NY 10012

MUSIC THERAPY AND RELATED ORGANIZATIONS

National Association for Music Therapy, Inc.
901 Kentucky Street, Suite 206
P.O. Box 610
Lawrence, KS 66044

Alliance for Arts Education
John F. Kennedy Center for the Performing Arts,
   Education Department
Washington, DC 20566

American Alliance for Health, Physical Education, Recreation
   and Dance
1201 16th Street, NW
Washington, DC 20036

American Art Therapy Association
428 East Preston Street
Baltimore, MD

American Association for Music Therapy
35 West 4th Street
New York, NY 10003

American Association on Mental Deficiency
5201 Connecticut Avenue, NW
Washington, DC 20015

Associated Councils of the Arts
570 Seventh Avenue
New York, NY 10018

Library of Congress, Division for the Blind and Physically
    Handicapped, Music Services Unit
Washington, DC 20542

National Arts and the Handicapped Information Service
Education Facilities Laboratories
850 Third Avenue
New York, NY 10022

National Committee—Arts for the Handicapped
Suite 801
1701 K Street, NW
Washington, DC 20006

OTHER

National Endowment for the Arts
2401 E Street, NW
Washington, DC 20506

National Endowment for the Humanities
806 15th Street, NW
Washington, DC 20506

Appendix **B**

COLLEGES OFFERING DEGREES IN MUSIC THERAPY

Alverno College, Milwaukee, WI 53215
Anna Maria College, Paxton, MA 01612
Arizona State University, Tempe, AZ 85281
Augsburg College, Minneapolis, MN 55454
Baptist College at Charleston, Charleston, SC 29411
California State University, Long Beach, CA 90840
Catholic University of America, Washington, DC 20064
Cleveland Consortia Schools, Baldwin-Wallace College, Berea,
    OH 44017
Colorado State University, Fort Collins, CO 80523
Dayton, University of, Dayton, OH 45469
Depaul University, Chicago, IL 60614
Duquesne University, Pittsburgh, PA 15219
East Carolina University, Greenville, NC 27834
Eastern Michigan Unviersity, Ypsilanti, MI 48197
Eastern Montana College, Billings, MT 59101
Eastern New Mexico University, Portales, NM 88130
Elizabethtown College, Elizabethtown, PA 17022
Evansville, University of, Evansville, IN 47702
Florida State University, Tallahassee, FL 32306
Georgia, University of, Athens, GA 30602
Georgia College, Milledgeville, GA 31061
Hahnemann Medical College (graduate only), Philadelphia,
    PA 19102
Henderson State University, Arkadelphia, AR 71923

Howard University, Washington, DC 20056
Illinois State University, Normal, IL 61761
Indiana University–Fort Wayne, IN 46815
Iowa, University of, Iowa City, IA 52242
Kansas, University of, Lawrence, KS 66045
Loyola University, New Orleans, LA 70118
Mansfield State College, Mansfield, PA 16933
Maryville College, St. Louis, MO 63141
Marywood College, Scranton, PA 18509
Miami, University of, Coral Gables, FL 33124
Michigan State University, East Lansing, MI 48824
Minnesota, University of, Minneapolis, MN 55455
Misericordia College, Dallas, PA 18612
Missouri at Kansas City, University of, Kansas City, MO 64111
Montclair State College, Upper Montclair, NJ 07043
Mount St. Joseph on the Ohio, College of, Mount St. Joseph,
    OH 45051
Nazareth College of Rochester, Rochester NY 14610
New York College at Fredonia, State University of, Fredonia,
    NY 14063
New York College at New Paltz, State University of, New Paltz,
    NY 12561
Ohio University, Athens, OH 45701
Pacific, University of the, Stockton, CA 95211
Phillips University, Enid, OK
Queens College, Charlotte, NC 28274
Saint Teresa, College of, Winona, MN 55987
Shenandoah College and Conservatory of Music, Winchester,
    VA 22601
Slippery Rock State College, Slippery Rock, PA 16057
Southern Methodist University, Dallas, TX 75275
Teachers College, Columbia University (graduate only),
    New York, NY 10027
Tennessee Technological University, Cookeville, TN 38501
Texas Woman's University, Denton, TX 76204
Utah State University, Logan, UT 84322
Wartburg College, Waverly, IA 50677

Wayne State University, Detroit, MI 48202
Western Illinois University, Macomb, IL 64155
Western Michigan University, Kalamazoo, MI 49008
West Texas State University, Canyon, TX 79016
Willamette University, Salem, OR 97301
William Carey College, Hattiesburg, MS 39401
Wisconsin–Eau Claire, University of, Eau Claire, WI 54701
Wisconsin–Milwaukee, University of, Milwaukee, WI 53201
Wisconsin–Oshkosh, University of, Oshkosh, WI 54901

BIBLIOGRAPHY

Cohn, Nik. *Rock from the Beginning.* New York: Pocket Books, 1970.

Cross, Milton, *The New Complete Stories of the Great Operas.* Garden City: Doubleday, 1967.

Furlong, William Barry. *Season With Solti.* New York: Macmillan, 1974.

Greer, R.D. *Design for Music Learning.* New York: Teachers College Press, 1980.

Hindemith, Paul. *Traditional Harmony.* Melville, N.Y.: Belwin Mills.

Jones, Leroi. *Blues People.* New York: William Morrow and Co., 1963.

Moore, Gerald. *The Unashamed Accompanist.* London, 1957.

Musical America: International Directory of the Performing Arts. Published yearly by ABC Leisure Magazines.

Newman, Ernest. *The Life of Wagner.* London, 1933–1947.

Pleasants, Henry. *The Lives of the Great Singers.* ew York, 1966.

Sadie, Stanley, ed. *The New Grove Dictionary of Music and Musicians.* London: Macmillan Publishers, Ltd., 1980.

Strunk, Oliver. *Source Readings in Music History.* New York: W. W. Norton.

Thayer, Lynn W. *The Church Music Handbook.* Grand Rapids: Zondervan Publishing House, 1971.